TRUST YOUR NEXT STEP

CREATING THE CONFIDENCE TO CUT FRESH TRACKS

KELLY ROBBINS, MA

M⊙tivational PRESS®

LEADERS IN GLOBAL PUBLISHING

Published by Motivational Press, Inc.
1777 Aurora Road
Melbourne, Florida, 32935
www.MotivationalPress.com

Manufactured in the United States of America.

ISBN: 978-1-62865-508-7

CONTENTS

To Shelby, Bailey and Madilynn Robbins.
My three amazing daughters.

THE FIRST STEP

It's time. It's time for you to take yourself on, to create your life your way. I call this cutting Fresh Tracks. Cutting Fresh Tracks is not for the faint of heart. It requires you to embrace your true self and take on a new challenge. To step into a new adventure. You know you are ready when you decide to take charge of *YOU* and begin creating different results in your life. You are ready to live your life your way.

You may have an idea of what you want to do, or just know something in your life is not right. Perhaps you have known this truth for quite some time and feel the purposefulness in achieving this step deep inside. And yet, you pause.

So what's stopping you?

Taking responsibility for your life and its outcomes is not the norm. In order to create a lifestyle, a business, health, love, happiness, and anything else you desire you will need to choose differently than you ever have before.

You may be choosing to do things that no one in your family has ever done.

Things like:

▶ Leaving a life of poverty and struggle
▶ Loving your body
▶ Working from home

- ▶ Traveling
- ▶ Feeling confident in your own skin
- ▶ Leaving a safe corporate job and doing your own thing
- ▶ Creating an online business
- ▶ Spending more time with your family
- ▶ Making double the money in your business
- ▶ Living your divine purpose
- ▶ Having more fun and adventure
- ▶ Stopping boredom
- ▶ Coming out of the spiritual closet
- ▶ Coming out of the sexual closet

I call this cutting Fresh Tracks. Why? Because you are stepping into an area of life and a space of creation that you never have before. But it's often bigger than that. We exist in a space we know and often become comfortable there. Our families, friends and acquaintances often reside in similar spaces.

It's called our comfort zone.

You may be actively involved in personal development and growth and find you are cruising along through life and are already surpassing many of the people you know in your family or career. Or maybe not. You may be completely miserable, have hit rock bottom, and are eager to be done with it with a fierce and burning passion!

Whichever place you are in, if you continue to push yourself and grow you will reach what I call "The Edge." The Edge is the very end of your comfort zone. Taking even one step past The Edge puts you in a place of creation, a place of newness, a place where you are creating life instead of reacting to it.

People often freeze right at The Edge and don't step past it. Sometimes unknowingly. Sometimes not. Often out of pure, unadulterated fear. Our unconscious mind, which is designed to protect us at all costs, doesn't want us to be afraid and comes up with logical next steps to help us avoid the uncomfortable position we are in. When you reach The Edge your potential next steps boil down to three options: take a step back, stop here frozen in fear, or to continue on past The Edge.

The first two of the three are safe and what everything in our body encourages us to do.

Going past The Edge can be terrifying and is usually incredibly uncomfortable. Most people will take a step sideways or a step backwards, allowing themselves to be distracted by a different, bright shiny object they think is moving them forward. In reality, they are avoiding stepping into the unknown. The unknown can feel soooo different and so uncomfortable. It doesn't feel right and your natural instinct is to avoid it at all costs.

Your first impulse may be to say "this is not me." However, if you find you have read just about every self-help book there is and have purchased several how-to formulas and kits to improve your life, such as: how to make more money, how to discover your purpose, how to start a business working from home in your pajamas and never have to leave the house...If you follow the formulas and yet are frustrated because they never work, or you frequently purchase another one before you finish the first, then you are avoiding stepping past The Edge.

There is a difference between acting on impulse and acting from your intuition. Acting on impulse is reacting without thinking about the consequences. Acting on intuition is acting based on a calm knowing from within. A knowing that comes from beyond your five senses.

In order to live a life of purpose and intention you have to step past the boundaries of your mind, past the invisible limits created by your subconscious to keep you safe, beyond what seems rational and logical and responsible, and start creating your own way.

You see, this is your life, it's your journey. And your journey is different than my journey. And it's different than your best friend's journey. And it's different than your mom or your dad's journey. And it's different than that famous guru you love so much.

You can learn from all of their journeys, but in reality, you can't follow in their footsteps—you have to create your own. If you haven't stepped beyond The Edge before, this may not feel safe. In fact, it feels scary as hell! It is incredibly uncomfortable and that's because you are going against everything everyone has taught you.

And yet… You know it's the right thing to do.

Because you are conscious enough to realize what you have been doing has kept you stuck exactly where you are right now.

And what happens when you do step beyond The Edge? In skiing we call it "going out of bounds;" going outside the safe and marked territory of the ski mountain. It's also known as back country skiing—just you on an open mountain where no boundaries even exist.

I assure you, the more frequently you cut Fresh Tracks the more confident you'll become. In fact you'll even become comfortable being uncomfortable—because that's where the growth is and that's where a life of purpose, intention and happiness resides.

When you are cutting Fresh Tracks versus following the trail of others, you'll see a huge difference in the results you achieve. In this space beyond the boundaries of your life you'll find that you can live your divine purpose. You will live a more fulfilled life and have the confidence that comes only from learning to trust yourself, listening to your intuition, and having the wherewithal to take your next step. You'll have created the life you truly desire.

Let's go cut some Fresh Tracks now.

CHAPTER 1

MAKING THE DECISION

ARE YOU COMMITTED TO PLAYING?

WHEN CONFRONTED WITH A CHALLENGE, THE COMMITTED
HEART WILL SEARCH FOR A SOLUTION. THE UNDECIDED HEART
WILL SEARCH FOR AN ESCAPE.

ANDY ANDREWS

Change starts with an awareness that something is not as you want it. Often people mistake that change starts with a decision—there is a subtle but important difference here. Making a decision is an important turning point in creating change. However, in reality, change starts with an awareness that you want something to be different.

You become *aware* a part of your life is unpleasant, uncomfortable or simply not how you want it anymore. As you examine this awareness, you become uncomfortable enough to explore options to experience life differently, realizing you have choices. After examination you set a clear *intention* of what you do want to experience. THEN you make a *decision* to create your intention. Finally you begin taking *action* to bring your intention into reality.

Awareness. Intention. Decision. Action.

Let's take a look at each of these four steps in more detail and what they mean to you as the creator of your Fresh Tracks.

AWARENESS

THE STATE OR CONDITION OF BEING AWARE; HAVING KNOWLEDGE; CONSCIOUSNESS.

Awareness is an under-discussed yet powerful tool for creating a purposeful life. Without awareness nothing changes. There are, for example, generations of women that have lived in unsafe, abusive situations and experience fear every day. They may leave that relationship and find another one very similar to it not soon after. They continue choosing unhealthy relationships because it's what they know. It's all they know. And it's all their parents knew and likely their grandparents and their great grandparents. Not only are these women unaware of how to make different choices, most are unaware there are any other options. Living in fear is the way their life is and always has been. Its familiarity, no matter how painful, makes it comfortable.

Imagine yourself trapped in a pitch black room. The room is so dark there is not even one sliver of light. Stuck in the dark room, there is no opportunity for exit as you can't see or even feel a door.

However, once a light is turned on, not only does the darkness disappear, but the light switch that was there on the wall all along can be seen. Light was always available, you were just a poor soul stuck in a dark room and weren't aware of the light switch. Once the availability of a switch is brought into your awareness, you will never be trapped in the dark again. You first must be aware of light and its possibility to look for it.

Achieving our highest potential is often outside of our awareness. We are so trapped within the box of what we can see with our physical eyes that we miss out on all the other wonderful possibilities available to us.

With that said, to create your own Fresh Tracks I invite you to first make the choice to be aware of what is possible. Choose to be aware of what you would like to change in your life. Choose to be aware of those secret, crazy-sounding, BIG dreams you don't share with anyone. Choose to be aware of what you would choose if anything was possible. You don't need to know how or have a reason why; you can simply choose.

So many of us go through life unaware of what is possible.

Imagine skiing at a ski resort. You have your map where the ski runs, boundaries and chairlifts are clearly marked. For most of us this is where our awareness stops. Some of us will focus only on where the green runs are. Others will scan the entire mountain and want to ski in one area or try all the areas of the mountain.

Most don't look beyond the rope, outside of the boundary. Looking outside the box or beyond the boundaries is not even an option because we are not supposed to look out there. Taking even the smallest peek beyond what you are "supposed to do" may bring up strong feelings of doing something wrong or that you are going to get in trouble for doing something you are not supposed to. No one wants to get in trouble!

Each of our families, communities, spiritual organizations, schools, jobs have these sorts of norms or boundaries. And we have become so accustomed to them that we not only don't question them, but we don't see them.

We go through life unaware of our self-imposed boundaries. It's difficult to cut Fresh Tracks from this space, because these are the runs everyone is skiing on, it's normal. This is where everyone resides and we are comfortable here where it's safe and familiar.

I am asking you to now be open to seeing beyond the ropes of your current life experience. Choose to see beyond the boundaries. Choose to be aware.

Personal Awareness

What to be aware of is a great question to ask. I would like to share with you eight qualities that are your birthright and that we all possess but may not be experiencing in some way. I was taught these are qualities of God energy. You can call them what works best for you. As you are exploring and defining how you choose to live your life and playing with what you want to create, know that experiencing all of these qualities is not only possible, but can and should be incorporated into every aspect of your life. They are:

1. Life
2. Love

3. Light (wisdom)

4. Power

5. Peace

6. Beauty

7. Joy

8. Abundance

Read each of these qualities and see what reactions they bring up in you. Does one bring tears of emotion or a sense of longing? Do you feel lacking in one or more of these qualities? Take some time and journal on each one and reflect on their presence in your life.

How can you become more aware? Here are some exercises to help inspire the process

- ▶ Journal
- ▶ Listen to your intuition
- ▶ Be aware of your breath as you let your thoughts wander
- ▶ Meditate
- ▶ Ask people you trust for feedback
- ▶ Participate in community spaces such as coaching groups, AA meetings, counseling
- ▶ Pay attention to your feelings and thoughts
- ▶ Write a manifesto
- ▶ Try to look at yourself objectively
- ▶ Perform a life review

Intention

AN ACT OR INSTANCE OF DETERMINING MENTALLY UPON SOME
ACTION OR RESULT. THE END OR OBJECT INTENDED; PURPOSE.

Setting your intention is the driving force behind getting you where you want to go. It sets the Universal Law in motion and empowers you in cutting Fresh Tracks. Everything that happens in the world starts with an intention. From clapping your hands, to calling a friend on the phone, to starting a business, it all starts with an intention.

Setting your intention is a powerful and important step in cutting Fresh Tracks and there is a correct way to do it. Think of your intentions as the seeds you are planting in the soil. If cared for, the seeds will germinate and eventually grow into the plant you planted. If you plant acorns you will grow an oak tree. If you plant strawberry seeds you'll grow strawberries. What can never happen is you plant pumpkin seeds and grow a rose bush. That is impossible.

If there are some things in your life you don't want, you've planted some weeds!

It's your job to be honest and open about your life and take responsibility for your results. What seeds have you been planting? Is there lack in your life? Poor relationships? Unhappiness? Lack of purpose? Are there weeds in your soil that need pulling?

Armed with these facts, be clear and specific about what you DO want to create.

Declare what you intend to create, and declare it with as much exactness and description as you can. Be specific. The art in setting intentions is in declaring what you do want without saying how it is to come about. What you don't want to do is say HOW this is going to happen, only what you intend to create.

Intention works best when you create from a place of calm centeredness rather than a place of lack or need. When you set your intention, know that what you desire is not only possible, but already happening right now. Do your best to feel into knowing it is real and done right now.

And then let it go. Release your intention, don't hold on tight to it. I find this the hardest of all the steps. This is where trust and faith come in. Holding on to your intention is like planting a seed and then digging it up every day to see if the roots have sprouted.

Let the intention go, yet take action steps towards bringing it into reality. In the seed example this would mean watering the soil, pulling weeds up from around the seed, making sure it receives enough sunlight and that it's not overheated or frozen.

Let's look at an example. Say you desire a new home. Your intention is to buy a new home, larger than the one you currently have by 1,500 sq. feet, in a better school district than the one you are in now. As you set your intention, clearly state which school district if you can, how many bedrooms, bathrooms, size of the yard, etc. Picture how your furniture will look in your new home. What are the neighbors like? What you don't want to do is declare HOW you will acquire the house. The HOW is the Universe's job, not yours. Your job is to clearly set your intention and then start taking steps to making it happen. In this example you might start house shopping, get your financing in order, find out what you need to qualify for a larger house, and start preparing your house for sale. Has the garage not been cleaned in five years and there is clutter in the spare bedroom? Take care of it.

Another terrific example of setting an intention without holding on too tight is how I manifested writing this book with my publisher, Motivational Press.

I had this book, *Trust Your Next Step*, brewing inside me for about two years. I hadn't paid much attention to it because I had started my podcast, *Fresh Tracks with Kelly Robbins*, and had been spending time growing into all that entailed. A business friend of mine asked me what I knew about publishing books because she had an idea for one. I have self-published a few books and have helped a few of my clients with the self-publishing process. She was asking about self-publishing versus going through a publisher and how to choose between the two.

As we were talking I shared a bit about my idea and it got me thinking, "What should I do with this book?" I thought about it for a while and remembered some advice my business coach gave me when making decisions like this—always step into the growth. Which choice is a growth for me? Working with a publisher certainly was as I hadn't done that before. So I set the intention that I would work with a book publisher. And then I did nothing.

A few months later, another business friend had a free ticket to a weekend workshop about self-publishing. It was two full days and packed with value and I said, "Absolutely, I'm there!" Sure enough, the workshop was fabulous. We both started writing our outlines and became writing buddies, checking in with each other every day to hold our writing commitments.

One day, while I was procrastinating on my writing, I googled "what's in a book proposal" and started writing mine. I read how publishers can hold on to your manuscript for months and not get back to you. How several rejection letters were normal and to not give up. To be persistent. I quickly had the outline and some of the main parts completed. Other parts I had no clue how to answer so decided I was better off getting back to work writing this book than spending time writing a book proposal—especially when I didn't even have anyone to send it to yet!

Meanwhile, I was still producing my podcast, meeting fabulous people across the world, learning about what they do and sharing their wonderfulness with my listeners. I was interviewing someone about her book and told her about mine. She offered to introduce me to her publisher if I was interested. Of course I was! This reminded me of my choice to work with a book publisher this time rather than self-publish.

Two weeks later I had signed my first book contract with a publisher that specializes in my industry and works with the authors to not only sell their books, but build a business behind it. As I opened the email and read the contract for the first time, a wave swept through my body. It was light, it was easy, and it was amazing! I realized what I had just manifested without even writing a miserable book proposal! I also sat in the realization that this is the exact same space for me to stay in to make a million dollars or accomplish any other goals I set my mind to. The exact same space.

Decision

A CONCLUSION OR RESOLUTION REACHED AFTER A CONSIDER-
ATION. THE ACTION OR PROCESS OF DECIDING SOMETHING OR
RESOLVING A QUESTION.

Living your life with intention and cutting Fresh Tracks is done one decision at a time. Our objective as creators is to get to the space where we are aware of what we want to create and we trust ourselves to know what step to take next.

You have to Trust Your Next Step without the security of seeing the entire path in front of you.

Security is a powerful force. A form of protection where a separation is created between an asset and a threat. Being a Fresh Tracker might sound completely amazing and reading this you may know it's exactly how you want to live your life. The truth is it's not an easy road because you are not used to living this way. There is no certainty and many folks feel afraid by the lack of security. How do you act when you are afraid? Most of us start out wanting to dip our toe in the water and see how it feels before we fully commit. We are out to reduce the risk.

Unfortunately, when you step past The Edge it doesn't work that way. You are either in or out and you have to make a "burn all the bridges behind you" decision that you are going out of bounds and you will follow this decision through to the end.

When you get married you are taking a risk. There are no guarantees the partner you choose will stay forever. No guarantee they will not develop addictive behaviors, love your kids, develop a mental illness, lose their job and become a couch potato you are stuck supporting… it's all a risk. How many people have that gut feeling they shouldn't be getting married before they walk down the aisle and don't honor it? Others step into marriage yet are quick to leave when times get tough. When you commit to a marriage you can plan and vision, but you don't know what the future will bring. It is a risk and the only way you can know if it's the right next step is to trust your intuition and stay committed to following through. It's about making a true decision.

How do you know you are ready to make a true decision? Here are a few signs you are ready

- ▶ You are at an incredibly low point in life and done with it (rock bottom)
- ▶ You are unhappy
- ▶ You are feeling bored
- ▶ You are looking for purpose in life
- ▶ The Universe made a decision for you (got laid off for example)
- ▶ A niggling feeling keeps poking at you and won't stop
- ▶ An idea, a yearning, a calling keeps coming up
- ▶ You are feeling stuck

HOW TO MAKE A TRUE DECISION

Most of us are not taught how to make a *true* decision. We think we know how to make a decision because we make thousands of them a day without much effort. The fact is most of these small decisions are habits, not decisions. They are automated and without thought. From choosing what toothpaste to buy to what clothes to wear for the day, generally we don't put much time or thought into our choices. We also make larger decisions, such as our New Year's resolutions or making changes to improve our health with much thought, yet we don't follow through with most of these and fail to stick to our decision to change. This cycle leads us to not trust ourselves. We don't believe our selves when we do make a declaration—and why would we? In the past we've never stuck with it!

This is because we are never taught how to make a TRUE decision.

A true decision requires three things:

1. Choice

2. Commitment

3. Urgency

Following these three steps allows you to make a *true* decision from a place of empowerment. And this where we start our journey.

CONSCIOUSNESS OF CHOICE

Oftentimes we feel stuck and it's because we don't think we have a choice. The truth is we always do! You may not like some of your choices but they are there.

Let's start with accepting that you *always* have a choice. Even when you are feeling stuck and trapped and can't see a way out, you have a choice.

Understand you ALWAYS have a choice, even when you don't think you do. Your choice can be to stay in the current situation. Maintain the status quo. Another choice is to do something different. Know there are options—you might not like some of the options, but there are always alternatives to where you are now.

For example, you may feel financially trapped in your job and because you have responsibilities you feel stuck. You may have a house, car payments, kids to raise and college to save for. Because of feeling stuck you are going through life numb, simply going through the motions each day rather than following your passions.

One easy way to bust through this step is to write out all your options. If you are struggling with seeing your choices, try to list them out by yourself first, then with a trusted friend. Lay out all of the opportunity you can see from where you are right now and just look at them.

Look at your choices, write them out, weigh your options with each one. Push yourself to write 25 or 50 different options. Then narrow them down to your top three. You'll probably find the first several are conventional and it's good to get them down on paper. The true inspiration and creativity may come later down the list.

For example, some of your options in the above situation may be to:

▶ Downsize your home in order to take a lower paying job you love

▶ Start taking classes on the weekends and evenings to transition into a career you do love

- ▶ Rent your house for a year, put everything in storage and move to Fiji for a year
- ▶ Move in your parent's basement temporarily while you launch your business
- ▶ Get up an hour earlier to write your book or go for a run

COMMITMENT

The second part of making a true decision is being committed to it. Do you have to have that "I'll do whatever it takes" attitude to cut Fresh Tracks? Yes, you do! This is where the important quality of commitment comes in. You'll need to be fully committed so you will continue to move forward even when you fail—which you will! Often. In order to commit fully to your success there is only one place to move, and that is forward towards your goal, one step at a time.

When you make a true decision and are fully committed to it, everything begins moving to bring forth your intention. To make your goal a reality. When I say "everything starts moving" be ready because it often starts with you needing to let go of what you no longer need in order to make room for the new.

It's important that you understand the Universe is always conspiring for your higher good. It's up to you to consciously take steps to grow in order for that good to come in. That means letting go of things BEFORE the new comes in. Not the other way around.

Here are a few common examples of movement:

▶ There may be people who need to leave your life to make space for new ones to come in.

▶ You may have to take action steps that other people will judge, and you may worry about what others will think about you (such as downsizing your house).

▶ You may be concerned what people will think if you make a mistake.

When you are truly committed you will continue to take steps in the direction of your decision even when you feel afraid and beaten down. It helps me to know that even when I am in a tough spot, the Universe is always conspiring towards growth and I, in fact, expect it to. When you are committed you play full-out and are all-in to achieve your goal.

THE BACKUP PLAN

When you make a commitment, you absolutely do not make a backup plan or a contingency plan. Having a plan B seems smart, however, in reality you are allowing not accomplishing your goal to be an option. Remember when you set your intention, you set it with the feeling and the knowing that it will come to fruition. A plan B is saying "if it doesn't…" Create from the space and commitment that failure is not an option. Period.

Here is an example of having a contingency plan that I'll frequently see with my clients.

They have the intention to start a business and will hire me to help them get it started—taking action in their commitment to live their lives their way. Yet, as they are working with me and starting their marketing and designing their pricing and packaging, they are looking for jobs at the same time. They spend their spare time scrolling though job boards and the classifieds "just in case" something good pops up.

When they do this they do not realize they have not fully committed to success in their businesses 100 percent. Sometimes it's unconscious and sometimes not. AND, because we know what you focus on expands, they are focusing on two outcomes:

1. Starting a business

2. Getting a new job

They are planting conflicting seeds and end up sabotaging themselves, struggling to achieve either outcome.

Building and Maintaining a Sense of Urgency

A sense of urgency is the final step in making a true decision. Success loves speed, and as such, you need to move swiftly and with determination. Urgency is something that comes from within and it's your job to cultivate it within yourself.

As a business coach, this sense of urgency is the toughest one to help clients with because you can't teach someone how to do that. I can't show you how to take something hard and make it take precedence over other areas of your life—only you can do that. Your job is to make your goals, your intention, cutting your Fresh Tracks, a priority. Developing a deep, burning desire inside you and cultivating that desire so it burns hot and stays hot is your job and your job alone.

You can be disciplined enough to go through the motions, but the passion and urgency required to maintain a state of being (loving, open, determined) is a feeling. Maintaining urgency and being motivated are about so much more than simply going through the motions.

For example, you can make yourself pick up the phone and call ten people every day. It takes urgency to pick up the phone and call ten people even when you don't feel like it. Even when it's already 5:00 and you didn't have time because your kids are sick. You can also pick up the phone and go through the motions of making ten calls, but your voice and energy is lacking and you have no passion or spirit in your voice. Can you see the difference? And how, especially as time passes, it can become difficult to maintain urgency?

When I made the decision to quit my corporate J-O-B and start my freelance copywriting business in 2000 I knew there was no turning back. The company I left did not hire people back once they quit. Ever. It was non-negotiable (bridges burned). On top of that, my desire to spend more time with my three daughters was incredibly strong. If I felt lazy or was stressing about where my next check was coming from, or was exhausted from being up all night with the baby, all I had to do was vividly remember the misery of putting on pantyhose each morning or my heart being ripped out when I dropped the crying kids off at daycare. I had to intentionally bring to the top of mind that sick feeling in my stomach when I couldn't leave work early to take my daughter to her Brownie meeting and indulge in the pain of how much of her childhood I was missing.

Sitting in the misery of any of those situations, and bringing myself to actually feeeeel the same gut-wrenching sickness snapped me out of my doldrums and right back on the phone making sales calls with a sense of urgency and determination. Anything I had to do, no matter how uncomfortable, was better than that, including cold calling!

It's your job to find what your hot buttons are to maintain urgency in cutting your Fresh Tracks. I see people struggle with this often and it's why so many people seem to fail. The truth is there is no such thing as failures—only quitters. People start things and don't follow through when times get hard or they get bored and just stop.

You have to master yourself and continuously fuel a sense of urgency and maintain it to cut Fresh Tracks.

ACTION

AN ACT. A DEED. SOMETHING DONE.

Taking action is the final and frankly the most difficult to maintain in the true decision-making process.

It's easy to get stuck and swirl around in the awareness, intention, and decision stages of creating Fresh Tracks. They are all important and each plays a valuable role in designing your future steps. The truth is that nothing will change if you don't move. You cannot meditate your way to success.

However, you also don't want to just start getting busy for being busy's sake. In the next several chapters we will get more specific on narrowing down your path and what direction to go.

For now what's important is that you recognize the importance of taking action and be self-aware enough to recognize when and why you may be avoiding it. Energy is built from energy. If you don't start moving you will not build the momentum necessary to cut your Fresh Tracks.

What I am going to teach you how to do is take small steps, one step at a time, focusing only on your next step. There are many ways to get to California from New York. There is not a "right way," there is your way and neither one of us knows what that is right now. We can plot and plan and project, but we won't really know until you actually get to California. Not comparing your journey to anyone else's is important. We get derailed when we become rigid in following other's paths instead of our own. Your tracks will include twists and turns and, more likely than not, be a winding road rather than a straight line.

Most of us want the straight, direct line to our destination and have techniques to avoid making a wrong turn. We don't want to waste time, money or gas on our journey! Procrastination is a common technique we use to avoid moving in the wrong direction and we start procrastinating when we are faced with fear or by how we might be shamed in some way.

Fear and shame are two of the biggest conditions that prevent us from moving forward in life and business. We are ashamed of what people might think of us if we fail. We feel ashamed to ask for help because we think we should be farther ahead in life than we are. We don't want to be exposed and vulnerable. We will do our best to avoid fear and shame by waiting until we see a safe and secure way to move forward.

There is a saying in my industry that many people striving for growth and consciousness are stuck on the "self-help shelf." The self-help industry is a two-billion-dollar industry and there is an endless supply of books, trainings and workshops to attend! Most of the population interested in personal growth reads a lot of books and may attend workshops and seminars to improve themselves. And yet, often after years of study, their lives have not changed in any way. They can talk the talk better than anybody, but they haven't walked the walk. They have knowledge intellectually, but have not physically embodied a change. Why? Because reading book after book after book is not taking action. Knowledge does not make tracks in the snow. Action does.

If you find yourself not taking action or feeling stuck, notice where you are stopping and get help if you can't see it. Seeing my own stuff can be the most difficult because I am in the middle of it all. I have hired coaches to more quickly and lovingly help me see what's right in front of my eyes!

A highly successful coaching client of mine had built her business through referrals for 20 years. In time, she had kids, moved out of state, and the business economy was changing in her market. She reached out for coaching, seeking guidance on how to move forward differently. She had a list of around 250 contacts—great contacts she had accumulated over the years. Yet, every time it came up for her to contact them she froze. She would create promotions and dig up new work with existing clients, but could not get past that invisible wall of sending an email or reaching out and calling each one of them. She saw where she was stopping and struggled to move past it. Why? Because her concern about what people would think of her was more important than increasing her income.

She also had an underlying fear of having too much work and not enough time for her family if her business grew, which took precedence over creating her Fresh Tracks and ultimately sharing her gift with more people. This is a legitimate concern and many of us can relate to it—family and our personal lives are important.

There are, however, many successful business owners who have balanced their family lives and work. The growth meant approaching life differently than she may have been exposed to in the past. Options for her included hiring people, outsourcing some of the work, relinquishing control of some of the processes, hiring people to do things around the house such as cleaning, grocery shopping and even walking the dog. Her belief that to be a good parent and good wife she needed to do those tasks for her family, rather than being open to other ways to show love, controlled the decision-making process and ultimately kept her in the same spot.

Taking an honest look at the actions you take, and taking notice of where you are stopping, matters.

Take steps daily, weekly, even monthly towards achieving your goal. Every small step counts. Don't allow yourself to be stuck in the planning, preparation, and research phase!

In-depth training from Kelly on Chapter 1 is available here: http://kellyrobbins.net/tynsadvancedmaterial/

The advanced material will give you access to a training video from Kelly, a recap of the chapter, a top tip from the chapter and a challenge for you!

You can also access our podcast here: www.FreshTrackswithKellyRobbins.com

Work along with the book in the *Trust Your Next Step Workbook* http://kellyrobbins.net/trust-next-step-workbook/

CHAPTER 2

DESIGNING YOUR PERSONAL TRAIL MAP: TRUSTING YOUR INTERNAL GPS SYSTEM

You have brains in your head. You have feet in your shoes. You can steer yourself any direction you choose. You're on your own. And you know what you know. And YOU are the one who'll decide where to go...

Dr. Seuss, Oh, The Places You'll Go!

Now you know how to create a change in your life—by first being aware of a discomfort, setting an intention, making a true decision to change, and then taking action—you are probably chomping at the bit to get going. Let's hold on for one more moment before you start plowing your way down the mountain out of control. That's when you start hitting trees or injuring yourself!

There are two main reasons people fail to create Fresh Tracks right off the bat:

1. In their excitement, they start running full force towards their goal, without taking a moment to assess where they currently are or where they truly want to go.

2. They plan. And plan. And plan. And plan. And plan. And never do anything. They don't take action.

I bet you know exactly which one of those two categories you routinely fall into. In cutting Fresh Tracks you will both create a plan and move full-force towards your goal—there is a balance between the two and that is where to focus your attention right now.

This book is called *Trust Your Next Step* because I believe we ALL know what our next step is on the path to cutting Fresh Tracks. The next step might be all we know, but we know it. You can trust it. It is your intuition and it is imperative you learn to discern your intuition from fear and from all the other voices from your past and present telling you what to do.

With that said, we are going to do some planning before we start taking action. We are going to create your personal trail map and there are only two points on this map that you need to know right now or ever.

1. Where you are right now. Your current location.

2. Where you want to go. Your destination.

YOUR CURRENT LOCATION

Defining your current location on the map is the first and most important step in moving forward. If you want to get to

New York and you just start walking, odds are you are going to go in circles or in the wrong direction. You have to know where you are. Are you in Louisiana? France? Australia? California? Quebec? You must know this before you start heading towards New York. How else will you know what direction to take?

Let's take this visual of a traditional map and apply it to your life so we can determine where you are. This can be harder to figure out than it seems at first because you may think you are in one spot but you are really in another. For example, when I started my first business I had these attributes: a bachelor's degree in marketing, 13 years' experience in a fortune 500 corporation, including experience in sales, marketing, working with a union, writing, and running a pricing department. I had three kids, a dog, a mortgage, a husband, and I lived in Colorado. I knew I was a good writer and I wanted to work from home.

That was how I determined where I was. In my mind my next logical steps were:

- ▶ Get a master's degree, because not having one was detrimental to me in my corporate position. OF COURSE I need one if I want to run my own business!
- ▶ Build a nice website and have a professional designer and e-commerce people help me.
- ▶ Buy expensive custom paper and envelopes, a logo and business cards. Because I am classy.

I was wrong here on several fronts. It took me five years in business and an extremely honest business coach to tell me the truth.

Here is where I really was:

- ▶ I had low self-esteem and no confidence. I needed to address that in order to charge the rates I needed to support myself.

- ▶ I needed to heal from an unhealthy relationship.

- ▶ My sales skills were incredibly lacking.

- ▶ I had to learn who I was and be okay with that. I had been people pleasing, being a good girl and doing what I thought were "all the right things." I was not being myself and did not know how to start.

Do you see the difference? How I was being was more important than what I did. Your location is not based exclusively on your credentials. Your resume. I did NOT need a graduate degree to run my business. I thought I was in Colorado on the way to New York but I was really in Egypt! I needed someone to show me that so I could begin taking forward motion from where I really was.

The truth was, no matter how fancy my website was or how much money I spent on custom letterhead, nothing was going to help me have confidence in myself when I asked for money to do writing projects.

My immediate impulse was to default to my credentials and the external things people would see. Clothes, letterhead, a fancy website—those things made me feel official. Qualified to serve others.

The fact is what's going on inside me plays a more important role in my success than anything. Earning more credentials and certifications, throwing money into external things such as products and websites is easier to do, and easier to see, than taking an honest look at the inner work that is screaming for growth and attention. That's why having an objective outsider (not your mom or dad) give you feedback can accelerate and clarify the speed at which you cut your Fresh Tracks.

Now it's your turn. Where are you starting on your map?

Start by listing your skills, interests, income, and family situation, anything you can think of that describes your current state.

► Debts, savings, training you've had.

► In what ways do you feel good about yourself?

► In what ways do you feel insecure?

► What does your support system look like?

► What is your personal development journey?

► Which relationships are healthy?

► Which relationships are toxic?

► Examine where you are from four sectors: physical, mental, emotional, and spiritual.

What is your 90-second, personal elevator speech? If you met someone new at a party, how would you introduce or describe yourself?

► As a mother?

► A lawyer?

► A yoga enthusiast?

► A single-father divorcee?

▶ A cancer survivor?

What are the stories that continually run through your head? Past your lips?

▶ Are you forever a victim of the economy?

▶ The deadbeat who left you alone with kids has you stuck at a job you hate because you have no choice?

▶ Your bad back leaves you home on the couch during your time off?

Where are you stuck and why? What if anything are you a victim of?

▶ The economy?

▶ Your ex?

▶ The IRS?

▶ Your parents?

▶ Drugs or alcohol addiction?

▶ Kids?

▶ Lack of money?

▶ Poor health?

Finding yourself is a powerful and selfless act that takes courage, openness and honesty. Knowing who you are, understanding what you value and what you have to offer in this world is a journey. Once you step into the journey you'll be capable of being the best partner, the best parent, the best you to offer the world in service. It is a journey each of us should take and involves letting go of layers of yourself that don't serve you in order to create the *you* you choose to be.

EXERCISE FOR DISCOVERING YOUR STARTING POINT

One way I have my clients get to know their starting point on their map is to write out their life story. Tell the story. Making sense of your past is one of the best ways to learn who you are and why you act the way you do. It's knowing your own story. As a coach I can read a life story objectively and am often able to point out holes or gaps in the story, bring to light patterns that may not have been noticed before, and help separate beliefs or patterns that may have been unconsciously adopted from parents who aren't healthy or don't support growth.

Research has shown that it's not just what's happened to us in our past that makes us who we are, but how we've made sense of it. How do you view what happened and why? Is there a healthier way to view it that will allow you to break some familial patterns? Increase your confidence and self-esteem? Are there some people you need to forgive?

Beyond the intellectual understanding of your history, there's the emotion behind some events that may need to be healed. If you feel a deep sense of obligation to attend every single event your child has, be the room mom of the century and volunteer at every party, feed the staff at every opportunity, and you know deep down that if you don't do these things you feel an impending sense of doom—it may make sense to look at why you feel that way. Why is this act so vital? Is it because deep down you feel like a terrible mother if you don't? Does that belief, even though it's not conscious, make moms who work bad moms? Do you believe that moms who are there sometimes but not other times don't care?

We all love our children and want the best for them. If you've got unconscious triggers and strong emotions around what is required to be a good mom for example, and starting a business and making money is in conflict with that, you will struggle.

Regardless of where you are now, you can change where you want to go. The map will change—but you always need to know your starting point. This means you have to know yourself—and this is its own wonderful journey of discovery.

YOUR DESTINATION

Where you want to go is the second point on your personal trail map. This is where you state what you intend to create. A health or fitness goal. A financial goal. A new job. Two weeks of world-wide travel every quarter. Writing a book. Your new business, etc.

There is power in clarity of intention. It's not enough to say "I want to take my family on a vacation this summer." Be specific, "I want to take my kids to Destin, Florida for five days and spend time at the beach, relaxing, snorkeling, and enjoying fresh fish all week." You can take it a step further by adding, "The kids will get along the entire trip, we will have more than enough money to do any activities we desire, and I will come home feeling refreshed and relaxed!"

The same clarity in your life goals and your career goals is necessary. For example, "I want everyone in the world to know that they, too, have the power to create their own Fresh Tracks" is clarity on how I choose to live on purpose and serve this world.

There are many ways to achieve this goal, but this is my ultimate destination. I have clarity on my "why" for being here. I believe that if everyone knew just how much power and choice they really have, we would all live our lives differently. Just think how the world would change! People would live on purpose, be happier and more joyful, and more pleasant and loving to each other.

Do you know your why? Your purpose? Now is a great time to stop and deeply think about this. If the purpose you first think of is what has gotten you in a big mess and you are stuck, I would like to suggest that is not your purpose. Your purpose does not need to be something big and lofty that sounds noble. You don't need to save the world. When I first started my business as a freelance copywriter my purpose was to have freedom of time. To have flexibility to spend time with my kids. THAT was my purpose and it fueled me to do things I didn't want to do but needed to. Such as make cold calls when I was tired and write my newsletter at 3:00 am to make sure it got out each week. Your why or your purpose is personal and you don't need to share it with anyone else. It can be selfish. It does not need to be important to anyone but you. Your purpose may be to put your kids through college so they don't have to work while they study. It may be to make your partner proud of you.

Similarly, a lifestyle goal may look something like this, "I intend to enjoy the freedom of working from home, have the flexibility to set my own schedule (i.e. take the kids to soccer lessons and volunteer at Brownies), and be able to leave for ski weekends a few times a month while making the same $5,000 a month income I did at my corporate job."

There are certain qualities that are pure, from Source, and our birthright to experience. If there are any areas of your life where you are not experiencing these qualities, or would like to experience them in a bigger way, incorporate them into your final destination. We journaled about these God qualities earlier and now may be a great time to use them to create your destination. These qualities are life, love, light, power, peace, beauty, joy, abundance. Consider how each of these qualities fits in your destination and embody where you want to go. How will you feel at the end of each day? At the end of your life, looking back, what do you want to have accomplished?

Take some time now to write with as much clarity as possible where you want to go. What is your ultimate destination?

Do not plot your course

Now that you've done this exercise your mind may automatically jump to fill the gaping holes and start climbing the huge mountains to close the distance from where you are to where you want to go. Do not let yourself get overwhelmed here because this is not your job right now!

Focus on plotting your map one step at a time. You don't have to plot the entire thing out now—because it's not your job to know step-by-step how you are going to get to your destination. Your job is to know your final destination with as much clarity as possible, and to get a good grounding on where you are starting from.

Here are a few suggestions to assist in relaxing and opening up to brainstorm:

▶ Go someplace where you do not usually work, such as your couch, the coffee shop, library, or back patio. Don't go where you normally pay your bills or do task-oriented business. Have a pad of paper or journal and write out your thoughts. Journal what your life looks like right now. What's working? What's not? What would you like to change? What/who are you happy with? Unhappy with?

▶ If you struggle with journaling, try writing out everything you dislike about your life or would like to change on the left side of a piece of paper. On the right side list the opposite of that.

▶ Visualize it. Many visual people like to create vision boards where you cut out words or pictures from magazines or find photos online. Sort through what you find and paste the best of the best to a poster board or piece of paper. What might your ideal life look like? Are there any themes? Surprises?

▶ Don't judge what comes to mind. Your dream may be that all your bills are paid and you are debt free. Perhaps you travel the world. Start competing in body-building competitions. Speak on stage. Write a book. Retire to the beach and serve margaritas to tourists. In the beginning, mine was being home with my kids and taking them to Brownies; I was not out to make a million dollars. What is true for you?

Not clear on your destination?

Not everyone knows where they want to go right away, they just know they are unhappy where they are. Many of us have been so busy struggling to keep our heads above water that we haven't spent much time dreaming about what we really want. Not only haven't we taken the time to think about the life we want to live, but we have been focusing on how stuck we are. We have stories about how negative our circumstances are and are unable to see a way out.

I've been there and it's completely okay to be in that space. You are AWARE something is not right and you are ready to use your intuition and step into creating change.

Your job right now is to start dreaming. What would your ideal life look like? Imagine you can accomplish whatever you want. Dream as if failure were not an option. Don't worry about HOW you are going to create your dream life, just take the time now to dream it.

If dreaming just brings up road blocks, start by writing down everything you DON'T want. What you hate about your job, your neighborhood, your relationships. Then write down the opposite of that. See how the opposite feels and again, while it may not be your final destination, it's getting you moving in a different direction and starting you on your path. I bring this up because one way I distract myself is by getting confused. I call it "going into confusion" and I do it over and over again. I can't see what's right in front of me and I make things way harder than I need to. That is one example of a road block. Also remember good things are often out of your comfort zone and you may not look there because it's uncomfortable.

KELLY'S STORY

When I quit my corporate J-O-B and took that first step into entrepreneurship I was not out to make a million dollars or save the world. My main goals in life were:

1. Flexibility to take my daughters to Brownies, cello and soccer lessons after school.

2. Make healthy dinners and feel good about how I was raising my daughters.

3. Never wear a suit and pantyhose again!

4. Make enough money to pay my bills.

I left my corporate job when my third daughter was born, realizing I was never going to have balance in my career or home life if I continued on the way I was.

I did not know how I was going to do this. I did not know what I was even going to do. I just knew I was determined to spend more time at home and failure was not an option.

Sixteen years and four businesses later, I can look back and know that yes, I accomplished my goals of creating my dream lifestyle. I worked weekends and early mornings, whatever it took—I didn't care as long as I achieved my main goal of being home with my kids. At the time, this was incredibly difficult for me to believe I could do. I am a mom with three kids. I don't consider myself super smart. At this point in my life I had finished a state college with less than a 3.0 grade point average. All I knew was that I HAD to make working from home work. Quitting my corporate job was scary and risky, yet it was a risk I had to take. Looking back, the only thing I really had going for me was my determination to succeed.

And evidently that was all I needed!

Of course, my dream lifestyle changed over time and I created new lifestyle goals for myself.

I encourage you to take the time now to think about what your dream life looks like. Dream as super huge (I'm thinking personal chef and private jet) or as comfortable as you feel. Don't judge your dream, just let it out.

What I've learned is once you achieve your current dream a new one quickly pops into its place and you continue to grow and evolve. Your job right now is to get started. Start moving, and as you move you can make decisions. "I don't like this. I do like this." Taking action, trying new things, and making mistakes is one way you can get to know yourself and start discovering what you DO want.

Use your internal GPS

Creating your personal trail map can be fun. However, filling in all the steps in-between—plotting out the map—is experiential. In this chapter we are creating a big-picture, realistic view of our life as it currently exists, and setting an intention of where we are going to take it. The goal is to recognize you have options. We all always have a choice.

We also innately have an internal positioning system that lets us know when we are on course or off course. When using the navigation system in your car you are familiar with the reality that if you go off course the GPS will let you know and automatically redirect you to the same destination by a different route. It's self-correcting by keeping with the facts of where you are and getting you to where you want to go via the fastest route. You may have changed the route, but the destination stays the same. I believe we all have an internal GPS that does the same thing, we simply need to learn how to use it and trust it! As you create Fresh Tracks it's important you master your internal GPS system through listening and practice. You have to learn how to use and trust your guidance system by knowing that you do know where to go and trusting that if you make a wrong turn your guidance system will automatically bring you back to the fastest route to your destination.

When you ski, the ski resorts give you a map of the mountain. Looking at the map it's easy to become overwhelmed with all the runs and opportunities to ski. Not only is there a wide variety of types of runs; greens, blues, black, double blacks, chutes, the terrain park, etc., but you will also quickly realize you cannot ski every run on the mountain in one day. You take the time to determine what kind of day you want to experience and plot out your course from there. Are you looking for a good workout? Want to ski a few easy runs and hit happy hour at the bar (Bloody Mary Happy Hour ends at 10:30am)? Is it a powder day and you want to go to less busy runs and enjoy the fresh snow while it's still there?

When you ski the more difficult runs with moguls, you are taught to "see the line" of the first few moguls and only then decide where you are going to go next. Imagine you are at the top of the run. Sometimes you can see the bottom, sometimes you can't, and you just start moving. Your intention is to get to the bottom of the mountain safely. From the top of the run you can't see every turn you will take. Even if you did plan your route, you have to remain flexible. Other people are also skiing and you may have to adjust your route to get out of the congestion. Or quickly get away from a few out-of-control folks skiing runs that are over their ability. You make decisions as the different conditions appear. The point is you start moving and see your next step just a few feet in front of you, knowing your end goal is arriving safely at the bottom.

Start at the top (where you are). Know you are going to the bottom (your destination). Ski each mogul, make each decision as you get to it. Trust your internal GPS system—you know what to do next. Planning too much ahead is an impossible waste of time and it is unlikely you can get down without having to make adjustments anyway.

Just like skiing the moguls, that is how you are going to create your Fresh Tracks in life, too.

In-depth training from Kelly on Chapter 2 is available here: http://kellyrobbins.net/tynsadvancedmaterial/

The advanced material will give you access to a training video from Kelly, a recap of the chapter, a top tip from the chapter and a challenge for you!

Work along with the book in the *Trust Your Next Step Workbook* http://kellyrobbins.net/trust-next-step-workbook/

CHAPTER 3

YOU DON'T HAVE TO STAY ON THE TRAILS

DO NOT GO WHERE THE PATH MAY LEAD, GO INSTEAD WHERE
THERE IS NO PATH AND LEAVE A TRAIL.

RALPH WALDO EMERSON

Right now your map has two points on it: where you are and where you want to go. We have left the "how to get there" blank and we are going to leave it open. Filling in the "how" is our next most natural instinct that I am strongly encouraging you to resist.

The next question to ask yourself is "What is my next step?" THAT is all you need to know right now. Listen to your intuition, in some instances you may need to be patient and see what appears, other times simply asking the question brings an immediate knowing—a whisper that must be honored.

Recognizing your next step

You may immediately know what to do next. Some of us have an internal knowing and it hits us right off the bat. We may not like what it is and try to think up something else—something better perhaps—to do next. This internal knowing or intuition may be a voice you hear. Others see pictures. Even others just know.

If you don't immediately know what the next step is, sit with it and wait for it to come to you. There are several different ways to let it come to you and we will review some of them now. Try different methods at different times and see if one works better for you than another. You may also find that one works today, and tomorrow a different approach is needed.

- ▶ Ask. Close your eyes and ask specifically what your next step is. And then just sit and wait. KNOW that you know what the step is. KNOW you will recognize it as it is presented to you.

- ▶ Draw your map visually, look at both where you are now and where you want to go and visualize what your next step is.

- ▶ Let it go. Ask, "Show me my next step" or make the statement "I have clarity on what my next step is" and then put it away. It will come to you in the shower or when you are gardening or doing something completely unrelated. I often go for a hike in the foothills of Colorado where I live and will have clarity after that. I find the mountains and being outside grounds me. Also hiking until I am exhausted moves my energy around—I release tension and worry—and opens me to seeing my next step. We often have great knowing when we do this method because there is power in letting go.

▶ Journal. There is a specific way I am going to teach you to journal, and while there is no right or wrong way, you can set yourself up to be more open by following this method. To start with, don't journal at your desk or where you do your task-oriented work. If you usually pay bills and answer business emails at the kitchen table, this is not the place to journal. Go outside on your deck, on the couch, your local coffee shop—someplace different where you can freely engage your creative juices and simply be in the flow. That's the where (or where not to) journal. Now the actual journaling…you can ask the question, "What is my next step?" and just start writing, fully expecting the answer to come. Alternatively, you can just write. Writing about anything that comes to mind is called freestyle writing. You might doodle words or incomprehensible sentences. Just keep going without judging until you feel complete. You may find you need to journal like this several days before the answer comes to you. Simply write, knowing the answers you seek will come.

▶ If you struggle with all of these and you feel stuck, hire a coach. Hire a good coach, not the cheapest one you find but one you feel a connection with and who has the skills to strongly and courageously call you on your shit. I know without a shadow of a doubt you DO know the answer to the question you seek. You DO know your next step, it is Universal Law that each of us knows this. You are either blocking it or don't see what's right in front of you because you are afraid. Or, you may not know how to listen to your intuition, which can take practice. Discerning between intuition and fear can take practice. An experienced coach can guide you.

WHY WE DON'T SEE THE ANSWER

Have you ever spent 20 minutes looking for your keys and it turns out they were right in front of you the entire time? This experience is called a scotoma, which is a mental blind spot. The truth is our beliefs shape what we do and do not see. They actually filter our perceptions. When you say "I can't find my keys" you actually gave your brain an "I can't" command—which it follows. You can command your brain in the same way by giving it "I can" commands.

In order to break out of this scotoma pattern you can:

1. Ask a question—what is my next step?

2. Ask the question differently—which path should I take?

3. Interrupt the pattern—hire a coach. Make a "burn the bridges" move and commit to breaking this pattern.

The answer you get, the nudge for your next step, will eventually take you to The Edge. This can happen on your first step or it might be on your tenth step. Beyond a shadow of doubt you will get there and when you do, you will be required to push yourself in an uncomfortable way and grow. You will be forced to make tough decisions and show your commitment to your desired outcome. Your subconscious knows this and, to protect you and keep you safe (which is its job), it will always find sneaky and insidious ways to block your progress.

Let's take a look at some common ways we block our progress:

THE RESEARCH TRAP

If you are anything like me and you are going to do something you haven't done before, you may want to learn more about it first. Research is often where people go next. You have a vision of starting a business as a yoga instructor—you know yoga but have never run a business or taught yoga before. Researching and learning best practices for running a small business is a natural next step before buying an existing yoga studio.

Let's say your goal is to become a competitive body-builder. Perhaps you've lifted weights and worked out for several years but don't know how to take your diet and exercise regimen to the next level. Research is a terrific next step. And it's the right next step.

When you research online you will find many "how-to" formulas, best practices, and often read about the journey others have taken before you. Depending on what you are doing you will probably find a lot of terrific information and insight.

You'll find many how-to kits and processes to tell you how to fill in the map and get where you want to go.

"How to make a million dollars online working from home in your pajamas," "how to hit the winning lottery numbers every time," "how to build a business in 90 days." While these sound great and the authors have good intentions, it can quickly become frustrating following other people's processes. You can follow many of these trainings to the letter and still not get the results they did. The bottom line is you have to figure out your way—it's your map and yours alone.

If you are analytical, more interested in reducing risk than moving forward, or simply keep looking for the "best" option no matter what, you are likely to fall into the over-researching trap. It's called analysis paralysis and it keeps you moving in a loop rather than taking action.

The truth is we have more access to quality information than ever before. Yet, rather than helping us make better decisions, this unlimited access leads to anxiety and a greater fear of making the wrong decision. Rather than trusting ourselves we look externally for answers and end up spinning our wheels, not moving forward.

If you have fallen into the too-much-researching-not-enough-doing trap, I recommend you research as much information as you can about your next step, put a time limit or end date on your research time, and then put all of that information away and start on YOUR journey fresh and open to possibility.

BEING TRULY ALIVE IS DONE OUT OF BOUNDS

You've made a decision that you want to do this—you are ready to cut Fresh Tracks. You are uncomfortable enough with where you are now that you are determined and ready to create a change. Then you began to plot out what you can on your map.

You did your best to determine where you are now and where you want to go.

The third and very important next step in creating your Fresh Tracks is understanding that you are the creator of your map. Your path will look different than anyone else's and that's how it should be.

This is your life. You have a unique background, different parents, beliefs, experiences, understandings than anyone else in the world. You are different and that is what makes you special. That is why it's so important you act from a place of creativity and energy and not simply going through the motions of what someone is telling you to do. Let's take a look at what it means to be out of bounds on the mountain.

In the ski world you can ski with a map and follow the trails the resorts have designed or you can ski out of bounds. It's a little scarier out of bounds—there is avalanche danger, your path is not marked with the level of difficulty of where you are going next, there are not safely posted and groomed trails, and finally, there is no guarantee you will reach the restaurant with the bar at the end of the run! However, skiing out of bounds is thrilling and one way to ensure you are able to create your own trail. It's one way to get away from the crowds, away from the groomed trails, and keep the out-of-control skiers at a distance.

Out of bounds the danger is higher, and the rewards are higher as well.

How can you ski out of bounds in your daily life? It starts with you determining you want to do something. Let's say you want to start your own business and work from home. No one in your family has ever done this, they've all had safe, secure corporate jobs their entire lives. None of your friends have done this either and you see them snicker when you mention it.

You feel strongly this is something you want to do, yet you don't see how you can do this right now. Because you are so determined you will figure it out. Based on your family and past experiences you will have to ski "out of bounds," break norms for your family and create this lifestyle for yourself. Understand taking these steps takes courage, and yet it is one of the only ways to heal yourself, change a family, and shift your life in a meaningful way. Making this decision will change your life and possibly the lives of others in many ways. We are all interconnected, and the change starts with you.

THE STATE OF THE LIVING NUMB

When was the last time you did something that scared the crap out of you? Something that, regardless of the outcome, left you feeing truly alive afterwards?

Whether or not you are better off because of the action isn't the point right now. What matters is the confidence and self-esteem you developed because you took that scary action, and that is what will stay with you forever. Knowing you have the capability, the wherewithal to play full out and just go for it is a strength builder. It is what makes us feel alive and not numb.

Most of us avoid stepping into this place because it is uncomfortable. And our mind, our ego, wants us to be safe and reside safely in our comfort zone. However good it feels, our comfort zone is also the place where numbness sets in.

I get very passionate about this topic of living a numb life because I unknowingly lived in this space for years. Going through the motions of life not feeling anything but doing all the right things is not being fully alive and living on purpose. It's incredibly easy to get stuck in this effortless no man's land. I believe over 90 percent of the population is going through life in a state of numbness and doesn't even know it because it's such a common space to inhabit.

What do I mean by living numb? It's going through life deprived of feeling or responsiveness. It's going through the motions of each day without passion or enthusiasm. Going to work, doing the laundry, watching television, getting the car washed, walking the dog, dressing the kids, checking Facebook… The busyness of surviving, keeping up with the Joneses, eking through our day-to-day routines allows us to avoid down time where we may just realize we are unhappy. We somehow effortlessly fell into living a purposeless life.

When you live numbly you don't feel. Many of us don't realize we are living a numb life because we are "doing" the right things on the outside, keeping ourselves busy and exhausted so we don't have time or energy to pay attention to how we are truly feeling.

You may love your children, feel proud of your state's football team (Go Broncos!), enjoy spending time with your friends once in a while, but as a whole your life lacks substance. When was the last time you felt the adrenaline that comes with facing a fear and pushing through a personal obstacle? The last time you felt the excitement that comes from using your creativity and trying something different?

This doesn't mean you need to become an extreme sports enthusiast to feel alive. This feeling can come from standing up for yourself when you normally wouldn't. It can come from asking for the raise you deserve. It can come from learning something new, such as taking a pottery class or embarking on a yoga retreat. From getting past day 21 in forming a new, healthy habit.

Have you ever fallen asleep on your arm and it gets tingly and goes numb but you don't realize you are in a bad position until it's too late? You realize you are uncomfortable, move, shake your arm around a bit to get the blood flowing again, and in a few minutes you are back to normal.

The same remedy can be used for shaking your life out of the numb state. The numb life is when your life energy is blocked or not flowing. We go through the motions of life not thinking for ourselves. Not dreaming. Not feeling. Shaking things around a bit gets the blood moving again in your arm and you can do it with your life too!

How do our lives become numb?

The truth is living a numb life sneaks up on us and can begin at an early age. It starts for some of us in school. We go to school because we have to, take classes we aren't interested in and simply go through the motions of what we think we are supposed to do to stay out of trouble. How many people do you know who finished their college degrees because they were supposed to, perhaps majoring in something sensible rather than careers they are passionate about? My business degree speaks to that!

I've spoken with many people, from medical doctors to nail technicians, who are in their profession because that's what their parents did, and continuing in their shoes is what was expected of them. They either didn't have the courage to stand up for what they wanted or didn't bother to take the time to figure out where their passion lies. They took the safe, easy road that didn't ruffle anyone's feathers.

And now they are among the Living Numb.

Years, even decades later, they are still living their lives based on what is expected of them. They are living their life because they want to please their families, their community, and other relationships more than they want to please themselves.

For most, the longer we continue engaging in people pleasing and living a charade, the more difficult it becomes to break through the shell of the lives we have created and become alive again. Responsibilities loom and we feel more and more stuck as we age. The house payment, the cars, the kids' sports and college expenses are all reasons to stay put.

We make excuses and tell ourselves "this is how it is." Statements like "work sucks and that's just how it is for everybody" and "I'll make do" or "it's not really that bad." Or we may tell ourselves we are "making the best of a bad situation" instead of addressing the underlying issue of not truly living a life of purpose.

Let's take a look at some common characteristics many experience in the numb life:

- ▶ Life lacks passion
- ▶ Stinkin' thinkin' is predominant
- ▶ Bored most of the time
- ▶ No longer dream
- ▶ Make plans that are routine
- ▶ Low energy or constant fatigue
- ▶ Don't want to hang out with other people
- ▶ Don't sleep well
- ▶ Have lots of ideas and nothing to show for it
- ▶ Not taking action on any dreams
- ▶ Life is incredibly busy so don't have time to think
- ▶ Can't think of the last time you did something for yourself
- ▶ Feel so much, so powerfully, had to shut down because it was overwhelming
- ▶ Frequently suppress the desire to express yourself
- ▶ Inactive, physically and emotionally, for a period of time
- ▶ Feel disconnected from other people
- ▶ No one gets you
- ▶ Don't know what you want and have just accepted what has come your way
- ▶ Feel empty
- ▶ Life is dull
- ▶ Feel in a rut

- ▶ Feel there is a void in your life
- ▶ Constantly striving to stimulate senses through sugar, alcohol, binge TV watching, drama or tumultuous relationships, working too much
- ▶ Constantly seeking validation
- ▶ Life lacks direction
- ▶ Living on autopilot
- ▶ Avoiding quiet time with yourself by scrolling through social media, email, etc.
- ▶ Days all blend together
- ▶ Frequently get to work and can't remember how you got there
- ▶ Eat lunch and don't taste the food

This list is fairly comprehensive. If you consistently feel more than five of these symptoms on a regular basis, it's time to shake things up and get on living!

Here's something to consider. If you feel nothing you are avoiding everything. The big scary decisions, along with the small scary decisions, may involve some pain. You may lose something or someone. It requires you to be vulnerable. In order to feel expansive joy, pleasure, and love, you have to become un-numb and be open and vulnerable to all of it. The good and the bad.

Disclaimer: *There is a fine line between going through life numb, going through the motions, and being depressed. If you think you may be depressed, get help from a professional.*

WHAT IS THE OPPOSITE OF FEELING NUMB? FEELING ALIVE!

Abraham Maslow was the first to recognize people have an inherent need to realize their potential. NOT striving for our potential is against human nature and is one of the main reasons we go numb in the first place.

Based on Maslow's hierarchy of needs, once your basic needs of food, shelter, love and belonging are met, self-esteem and self-respect become important factors to our growth and happiness. Followed by self-actualization. Maslow describes self-actualization as *"The desire for self-fulfillment, namely, the tendency for you to become actualized in what you are potentially. This tendency might be phrased as the desire to become more and more what you are, to become everything that you are capable of becoming."*

Intellectually that may sound great. To become everything I am capable of becoming. Who wouldn't want that?

Remember all the times you thought your company wasn't using you to your fullest potential? The relationships you so desire yet struggle to make? The money you KNOW you are capable of making "just if?"

The truth is that actions have to take place for us to create this life. This feeling of being alive. The numbness sets in because of inaction. Giving up is stopping the action. Reading every self-help book written is not enough action to feel alive. Watching positive and informative Ted talks or trainings for hours doesn't quite cut it either.

Let's take a look at some of the characteristics of someone who is living in a self-actualized state. Someone who is truly enlivened and embracing life:

- ▶ Does what they love
- ▶ Feels—both ups and downs
- ▶ Knows that "it" is possible—whatever "it" means
- ▶ Feels excited frequently
- ▶ Passionate about one or many things
- ▶ Takes action in spite of fear
- ▶ Looks inside for answers
- ▶ Trusts themselves
- ▶ Does not people please
- ▶ Sees opportunity around them
- ▶ Takes action towards achieving goals
- ▶ Puts themselves first
- ▶ Sees a higher purpose in life
- ▶ Has friends and a social group
- ▶ Makes decisions based on what's best for them, not others
- ▶ Sees opportunity at every corner
- ▶ Spends time with themselves
- ▶ Is present
- ▶ Achieves goals
- ▶ Is open to receiving

Would you like to have more self-actualized traits than numb traits? Try taking one or a few of these action steps and see where it leads you!

Here are some first steps you can take to snap out of the Numb State and start on the path to living on purpose:

- ▶ Change the questions you ask yourself. Ask empowering questions requiring open-ended answers.

- ▶ Become aware of your feelings. You can do this in several ways, including journaling.

- ▶ Start paying attention to what does grab your attention and ask why.

- ▶ Talk with friends who you feel are living a life you would strive for.

- ▶ Do something different. Anything.

- ▶ If you have an idea or dream you've been thinking about for a while, take action towards achieving it.

- ▶ Be around different people. Meetup.com is a great place to find a hiking group, book club, or meet entreprencurs.

- ▶ Pay attention to your gut, your intuition. Your intuition only speaks to you in positive messages. If you hear or feel something negative, it is fear. Your conscious mind is different than your intuition. It can take some practice and attention to learn the difference between the two.

Snapping out of the numb life and entering into the land of the living again is a journey. The road is winding and there will be times when it feels like you take a few steps backwards as you inch your way forward. That's to be expected.

Overall, there are two main things you are striving for internally on the path to feeing alive:

1. **Trusting yourself that you** DO know what the next step to take is. The only way to build solid, unwavering trust in yourself is to begin paying attention to your signals—however they appear. A gut feeling. Hearing the same thing from different people. Dreams. And then start taking steps. If you don't move you won't go anywhere. You HAVE to start taking action steps, small or large doesn't matter, in a concerted direction. Odds are, the movement will vary from incredibly uncomfortable to incredibly euphoric.

2. **Creating Fresh Tracks**. This IS being alive. Living and creating your life your way. Living and doing what you choose to do how you choose to do it. Creating and expressing yourself to the fullest extent possible. And then doing it again. And again.

I didn't realize I was living the numb life until after I started feeling again. I had been unhappy for a long time, busy raising young daughters and struggling with the ups and downs of growing my copywriting business. I saw an opportunity to take a free meditation class. I had always wanted to try meditation and jumped at the chance! I signed up for the five-week class, which seemed to go excruciatingly slowly, but I wanted to continue practicing meditation and I was curious about what else there was to learn.

There was a group of about eight or nine of us and we learned to ground ourselves, clean out our aura and chakras, energetically protect ourselves from others and we practiced feeling. Which sounds odd at first, but many, including me, found it quite difficult. We started by feeling different colors. What does yellow feel like? Blue? Green? It was fun, definitely different, and it felt good for me to do something for myself that had nothing to do with kids or work or the house.

I ended up taking classes at that studio for two years. I strengthened my intuition, energetically worked through a variety of issues, and learned to energetically read, heal and assist other people. Looking back, the biggest thing those classes taught me was to start feeling again. I didn't realize I had stopped. I had been unknowingly living a numb life for years and it took feeling orange and blue to start snapping out of it!

Being numb is a common occurrence that creates blind spots in our growth. What are some other backdoor ways we sabotage our ability to cut Fresh Tracks?

Sneaky self-imposed obstacles that block our progress

THE GOOD GIRL/GOOD BOY SYNDROME

Most of us were raised to please, to conform, to fit in. Standing out from the crowd or being different than our community is not traditionally embraced. In fact, many of us were shunned or punished for not fitting in. We were bullied, ostracized, made fun of, grounded, swatted and more.

When we are cutting Fresh Tracks it's going to feel like the exact opposite of everything you've been taught to do and most of us feel incredibly uncomfortable once we step into it. Recognizing uncomfortable feelings when they come and deciding to keep them or not is a key factor to moving forward and not stopping frozen in your tracks.

I was raised with the belief that getting the right job, a custom home, 2.5 kids (the rebel I am, I had 3 girls!), being in the right school district and driving the right car are symbols of success—and this is what I was to strive for. When I shared with my family I wanted to quit my corporate job and work from home, my family advised me strongly against it. Their reasons sounded legitimate and I know they had my best interests in their heart. However, the corporate path was not the right one for me and I had to trust myself.

Going to work in a corporate setting, I was always on guard. Office politics kept me nervous and constantly focusing on what the right thing to say and do was. Even my work had to be approved by a committee and legal department. I didn't feel as if it was acceptable to be myself and, rather than spending time discovering who I was as a young adult in my 20's, I concerned myself with being who I thought I was supposed to be. And while I may not have been able to articulate that at the time, I did know my life wasn't working. I didn't trust myself, I was shy and would be quiet rather than stand in my power. I was a good girl, did the right thing and tried to stay out of trouble!

Can you relate? If not at work, in a relationship? In regards to your health? Understand that all of this conforming has been going on since we were young children in school. And we act and respond and create our life from this conforming space—mostly unconsciously.

One of my favorite books is by the author and composer Robert Fritz called "The Path of Least Resistance." In the book, he talks about how we are raised to solve problems rather than create what we actually want to experience in life. For example, an artist doesn't solve the problem of a blank canvas. A musician doesn't solve the problem of the blank page. They create their vision.

When you create Fresh Tracks, I challenge you to not solve the problem of not enough time, but create more time to do what you enjoy. Don't solve the problem of not enough money to pay the bills, but create abundance and freedom in your life.

When you look at your map and get to the uncomfortable space where you haven't been before, your mind is going to default to "solve the problem" mode. That's what you have been hammered to do since you were a young child in school.

I am going to ask you not to do that. I am going to ask you to listen to yourself, trust your intuition, and make a step from there. Trust your next step. Put your mind on what you want to create—the positive.

JUDGING WHAT WE WANT

If you want something you want something; don't judge it. A judgment is an opinion, either good or bad. It's possible to get to the place where you see or feel something and recognize it just "is." It's a feeling, it's not good or bad. Recognize most self judgement is automated and it often happens faster than we realize. What can you do to prevent judging? Start by taking the time to be aware of your thoughts and reactions as you dream about your future life. We tend to be our own worst critics and it is a self-destructive habit.

It may help to understand you wouldn't have the idea to want it if it wasn't spiritually guided. Even if it seems ginormously out of your range of accomplishment right now, you wouldn't have the idea unless you had the ability to manifest it. I'm not saying it will magically and effortlessly appear on your doorstep tomorrow, but if you start right now, start taking steps in the direction of achieving what you want to achieve, you will. It's important for you to not judge your dreams. It's also just as important that you don't give others the opportunity to judge them. Particularly family and friends that may be well-meaning can do more harm than good.

Hidden unsupportive beliefs

The more you get to know yourself and stand confident in what you believe in, the more you'll find that you hold onto beliefs that don't support you. I often see these around money. Many of us raised in middle class America heard statements growing up like "Money doesn't grow on trees," "He's filthy rich," "A dollar saved is a dollar earned" and more.

As you continue down the path creating your Fresh Tracks it's your job to dig up and recognize hidden unsupportive beliefs that are blocking you. They are not usually easy to spot! I had a client, Diane, a wonderful woman who started a transformational coaching business. She was incredibly talented and an impactful speaker, workshop leader and coach. She hired me because she was struggling with her marketing and ultimately making money in her business. She wanted help with creating her website, creating her marketing funnel, and ultimately increasing sales. As we began working together I uncovered she had been agonizing over finishing and launching her website. For two years! We talked about it and I had her show me a few websites of other people in her industry and what she did and didn't like about them.

What she came up with was insightful. She didn't want to be pushy or a showoff. She didn't want to brag. She didn't want to be loud. We discussed how, as a business owner, particularly in her field, she needs to be seen and people need to hear her so they can find her. She can't be a quiet mouse hiding in the corner keeping her beliefs to herself. Where did these hidden beliefs come from? Her childhood. Her ex-husband. Her desire to fit in and not rock the boat to stay out of trouble. Don't get me wrong, Diane came from an incredibly loving and supportive family. These values and beliefs are often so hidden in our culture that we don't recognize them until we reach a point, like Diane did, where you just get stuck and can't move past it.

Once Diane examined her beliefs she was able to move past them quickly, had her website up in two weeks, and filled a workshop. Diane realized you can't make an impact in this world and change lives if no one can find you. Her hidden beliefs about being seen were impacting her ability to connect with people and make money in her business.

Distractions…Avoiding the bright shiny object syndrome

For those of us who have too many ideas to keep track of, we often start on one path and half-way through (or when it starts getting hard) we find something "better" that will take us to the same place. I see this most frequently with entrepreneurs because they tend to generate ideas 100 times faster than the rest of the population, and each idea is better than the one before it. There is an excitement and adrenaline rush in starting something new and for some of us it feels much more comfortable and fun starting a new adventure than trudging through the second half of a project when you may not be seeing its full results yet.

What I do to help combat this disruptive habit is keep my goals written on a sticky note next to my computer—it helps me keep them top of mind. For my clients, we keep them at the top of a form we review before we have our coaching calls. Before spending money on anything, stepping into a partnership of any kind or adding more training or advice on a topic, stop, take a few deep breaths, and see if your desire is taking you closer to each or all of your goals. It's easy to convince yourself you need more training when you really just need to finish up what you've started, so be careful!

Final advice for getting off the trails

I want you to hear me and take this to heart. This is your life and you have the choice to live it your way. This is not your mom's life. It's not your spouse's life. It's not your kid's life. You get to choose how to live it. There are many people's voices in your head speaking to you all the time and telling you the right and wrong steps to take. You have to own this…it is your job and only your job to quiet those voices and learn to listen to your voice alone.

First, recognize who's who in there yapping away and then kindly shine the light on them and ask them to leave. Sometimes a therapist can help with this. I believe spending a year delving deep into learning about yourself and why you do some of the things you do is an important part of your journey. Having a professional guide you through the process can be healthy, and in fact can speed your growth by leaps and bounds. I'm not advocating that everyone needs therapy. But having a professional help you see who you are and how you got there can speed up the learning curve in many ways.

Change is growth, and growth is always a reach, a step up the ladder. It's not sideways or backwards or standing still. Your natural inclination is going to be to turn away from fear, to avoid the unknown you are challenging yourself to step into. Particularly when you get to The Edge. That's why it's so important you recognize The Edge when you get there, so you can make a conscious decision to move forward. Don't let hidden, unsupportive beliefs, blind spots and destructive self-judgment block your way.

In-depth training from Kelly on Chapter 3 is available here: http://kellyrobbins.net/tynsadvancedmaterial/

The advanced material will give you access to a training video from Kelly, a recap of the chapter, a top tip from the chapter and a challenge for you!

Work along with the book in the *Trust Your Next Step Workbook* http://kellyrobbins.net/trust-next-step-workbook/

CHAPTER 4

RECOGNIZING THE EDGE AND STEPPING PAST IT

What is The Edge and why is it there?

Many people recognize The Edge as the end of their comfort zone.

Here's a definition of comfort zone from Wikipedia: The *comfort zone* is a psychological state in which a person feels familiar, at ease, in control and experiences low anxiety and stress. A behavioral state where a person operates in an anxiety-neutral position.

As you embark on creating your Fresh Tracks my bet is you will not be in an anxiety-neutral position! There is no growth in the place where you feel familiar, at ease and in control. I believe we are here, alive on this planet, to grow and expand.

I would bet you have set goals at one point or another in your life. And if you're like me at all, there are times (many times!) you didn't accomplish them. Why didn't you accomplish them? Because it gets hard! You get lazy or bored. You don't want to do what you need to do next. Basically you became uncomfortable and stopped.

Imagine how different your life would look if every time you became uncomfortable you moved faster and pushed yourself harder rather than stopping and turning around because of discomfort? What would happen if instead of stopping when you become uncomfortable you are so accustomed to the feeling you embrace it? You seek it out rather than avoid it?

My challenge to you is to expand your comfort zone to the point where you are accustomed to reaching it and pushing past it so that each time you do reach The Edge it's not such a shock to your system.

It's easier for you to continuously create Fresh Tracks if you can become comfortable being uncomfortable.

Most of us spend the majority of our time inside our comfort zone, and the truth is that zone is pretty small. Increasing your range of comfort by stretching and expanding your comfort zone allows you to remain stress-free and comfortable more often. You can do this by intentionally putting yourself in situations that make you uncomfortable. Continuously putting yourself in uncomfortable situations allows you to build the confidence that you can and will successfully make it through and past your fear. When you start to say to yourself "I've never done this before," you'll get a positive charge rather than a negative.

Rhonda Britten, founder of The Fearless Living Institute and author of *Fearless Living* teaches there are three levels of stretching your comfort zone. There's a stretch, a risk, and a die. A stretch, Britten says, is something we know we would be better for doing but aren't doing it. An example could be spending less time on social media or watching less television. Things you know you can and should do, but instead, tend to be lazy and beat yourself up for not doing.

A bigger way Britten shares to expand your comfort zone is taking a risk—a risk is something you're not sure you'll be successful at. When you take a risk you may think you can do it but have a "what if I suck?" kind of feeling.

And the biggest and fastest way to expand your comfort zone is a "die" for a stretch. A "die" feels like a crazy choice and makes you shake in your boots at the thought of it. Your immediate response is "No WAY!" when asked. Examples of common dies are public speaking or sky diving.

You can stretch your comfort zone a little bit at a time or in one big push, and your Fresh Tracks are created as you do it! Fresh Tracks are not created within the safe, comfortable place you spend the majority of your time. Fresh Tracks enliven you and are ultimately what lead you to living the life you choose to lead.

WHY WE STOP AT THE EDGE

Why do some people accomplish their goals, cut Fresh Tracks, and live a life of happiness and fulfillment while others are stuck living a numb life, never creating or expanding themselves?

Because most people stop exactly at the point where they can't stand the fear (pain) anymore. They stop where the discomfort in stretching themselves past The Edge becomes so unbearable, staying where they are is more important than taking the steps they had set out to do. The truth is everyone's tolerance for pain is different, both physically and emotionally. I have three daughters and each of them has an incredibly different tolerance for physical pain. My oldest, Shelby, has zero tolerance. Even when she was an infant she couldn't handle pain. Every tooth brought on a fever and sleepless nights and crying. It hurt! Her younger sister, Bailey, can handle much more pain. Many of her teeth popped in unnoticed. I watched her crash her bicycle and bruise herself and quickly pop up and move on with her agenda.

Here I am using physical pain as an example because it's easier to see and compare. Our limits in pushing past our fears are not always as easy to see.

What is your tolerance level and how can you recognize where you stop?

We generally have two overriding reasons for stopping cold in our tracks:

1. Frozen in Fear. We consciously make a decision not to step into a growth because of fear. We know what we are doing (or not doing) and make a decision to turn back. We may tell ourselves it's our gut telling us to turn around and we are trusting ourselves, but most of the time it's fear. Understand that intuition only speaks to you in positive terms. Negative nudges are usually fear. In these instances we are using our intuition as a scapegoat. When we are expanding

at a high level we may not recognize the difference between fear and our gut and it can take practice to learn the difference.

2. Can't see past The Edge. People don't go past their edge because they don't even know they can. Taking another step is not an option because they're not aware that stepping beyond what they've always known is even possible. The world was flat until someone sailed around it and discovered it was round. No one ever imagined it was round. People believed it was flat because the experts said it was flat.

Let's take a look at some examples of how this happens in everyday life:

A client of mine, Terry, a mother of five, had been struggling to make more than a few hundred dollars a month as a writer and public relations consultant. She was incredibly talented and had many years of experience. She struggled with life balance. Giving herself permission to enjoy her work and be a good mom at the same time was a challenge. It was very important to her (and her sanity) that she maintain her writing and communications career while raising her kids. She just wanted to make more money at it!

Realizing she was stuck and frustrated, she hired me to help her see past The Edge. Where was she stopping? With a lot of tears, work, and pure guts, she created Fresh Tracks for herself and her entire family by setting boundaries with her kids, letting go of several volunteer positions that no longer served her and renegotiating rates with her clients. Within six months Terry had raised her rates from $25 an hour to $75, let go of a few clients who were more trouble than they were worth, and by making a few phone calls, managed to find a few new clients that brought in a higher rate and added a fun, fresh feeling to her work.

Why was Terry successful when so many aren't? She was open to honest feedback and was willing to honestly look at herself and her beliefs. She knew how she had been "being" was getting her the results she no longer wanted. Terry had to see herself and the value she offers the world in a truer light than she had been, and at the same time strengthen her spiritual self-esteem that she WAS worth raising her rates and worthy of living the lifestyle of her choice. She didn't have to be super-mom to triple her income and raise her family the way she choose.

Terry looked at her belief that she was worth the going rate and not less because she worked from home. Terry asked for help from family members and set boundaries with her kids when she really didn't want to. Terry had healthy relationships and a supportive partner who helped her achieve her Fresh Tracks.

MY FROZEN-IN-FEAR STORY

About two years after I had begun my healing journey, I delved head first into personal development. Learning about who I am and why I act the way I do and how to achieve my goals were my main missions in life. I attended seminars, I hired coaches, and I pushed myself to try new things that scared me in order to grow. I did it consciously. After a solid year of delving into the healing of Kelly, my business grew, I was making new friends I enjoyed spending time with, I was happy. I found myself dancing and singing in the kitchen when I made dinner and just having fun. Life was great!

And then, about two years later things started to slow down for me. Business slowed down, my relationships weren't as fruitful as they had at first been, and I found myself wanting to hide out at home more (I am at heart a homebody and introvert and love curling up at home with a good book). I knew something was going on, so I signed up for a personal development seminar my friends had been raving about. This one took me to a ranch in California for seven days.

I knew it was different when they took my cell phone away for the entire week...

I had never been to anything quite like this before. There were rope exercises and wiggly poles we climbed and had to jump and grab a trapeze in midair. The exercises were designed to push us so we could learn more about ourselves in situations that we weren't familiar with. The situations were designed to be raw, where we didn't have a history to default to a correct way to behave or react. Most of the exercises scared me to death.

There was one exercise that stood out from the rest... it involved me walking partially up a mountain. Unlike the other exercises, I couldn't see what this entailed before I got there. As I was going up, some of the group was walking down, laughing and seeming like they had fun. It was my last exercise of the day and I chatted with my friends as we walked and wasn't too worried. We were stopped at the bottom of a steep trail with a bunch of jagged rocks above us and told to leave our backpacks and all of our stuff at the bottom and proceed up the trail individually. It was beginning to bother me that I couldn't see what was going on. The other events I had been able to watch a few people go before I took the leap and could prepare myself for the fear.

I wiggled through the rocks and got to the top and saw two distinct groups. I was swiftly directed to the group on the right. I walked right up to a man who put a harness on me and pointed me to a small, wiggly looking plank that hung over the edge of a cliff with jagged rocks below. They expected me to walk to the end of the wiggly looking plank and hang over those jagged rocks, with only a harness holding me in place, held by a man—an older man—holding a measly little rope! My knees were shaking as he explained to me what I was to do. I nicely asked if I could go later after I watched a few people go so I could see how it worked, and I was told resolutely, "No!"

My hands were shaking as I stood looking at the plank I was expected to walk down. There was no turning back, so I just started edging my way slowly down it. I was so afraid I plain and simply started bawling.

I was petrified. The plank was shaking and there was no way I was going to do more than stand at the edge. I did get close to the edge and realized I was thousands of feet up in the air suspended by a rope on a wiggly old wooden plank! I just couldn't move. The man called me back, hugged me, and started talking to me.

He told me this was an exercise about trust. Did I have a difficult time trusting people? I didn't think so, but clearly by my extreme reaction to this particular event I did! He explained that I only got one try at this event, and this was my special opportunity to face myself head on and break through my fear of trust. He was the owner of the company and had been doing this for 25 years and never once has anyone been hurt. Would I be willing to try this again?

He was so nice and talked to me through my tears so kindly. I had to say yes. And I was, after all, there to change my life.

I walked out to the edge of that shaky plank, sure that was I going to slip off the side. I got to the edge, still crying, and didn't know what to do! Really, how does one just lean forward? It's not a natural position. I did finally figure out how to lean a little bit and I heard the crowd roar.

Some of my friends (who had already completed the exercise) were watching and encouraging me on. As I leaned over the edge, looking at the hundreds of feet of jagged rock below me, I knew I could conquer anything. The man encouraged me to yell some things out to the open vastness of the California countryside that I wanted to let go of. I was barely breathing, so screaming words out to the Universe was not going to happen. I felt myself drop a little lower, which was scary but I was doing it. He continued to talk to me and after what seemed like hours I came back up. I was SO proud of myself. I went back to the group that had finished the exercise with the shakiest legs I've ever had, happy to be breathing and alive, and watched the next person come up.

I was very interested to see how the next person did and let me tell you I'm glad I watched. She did not get half way down to the plank when she turned around, said no way and took off her harness and walked off, not even trying the exercise. She was having none of it and I can't say I blame her!

To my astonishment the man motioned me back up. He put his arm around me and said something I will never forget. He said "See what just happened. She turned back and did not face her fears. And that is different than what you did. You remember what you are made of. You keep going." I will never forget what he said to me because I did see how I faced my fear—and it was real—and I had leaned forward on the plank in spite of myself.

Now I was curious to keep watching. The next person came up, walked down the plank happy as could be, and that lady laid out as flat as the ground not concerned one bit about the jagged rocks below her. She was yelling and releasing to the Universe at the top of her lungs how happy she was. I know my mouth dropped open in awe at what was actually possible! I guess trust wasn't an issue for her!

I have a picture of me doing the trust event in my office to remind me of how it felt for me to conquer my fear and cross that Edge. The funniest thing is in the picture I am barely leaning! The picture doesn't look scary to anyone looking at it, but I remember the feeling that came with hanging over the edge and I try to remind myself to push to that edge every time I get a chance, because that's where I'm alive and that's where the transformation takes place. Incidentally, this exercise was called "The Edge."

My hope is that as you step into creating your Fresh Tracks you will also face your fears and step into them rather than say no, like so many others, and turn around and walk away. It's not what we are here to do.

THE LENS YOU SEE THROUGH

How you view the world plays an important role in cutting Fresh Tracks. What you believe will happen or could possibly happen is often what DOES happen.

We each have our own lens we view the world through. Our family, our heritage, spiritual influences, the community we were raised in, our past failures and successes all play a role in how we see the world. Pessimistically. Optimistically. Cautiously. Powerfully. Fearfully. Shamefully.

My client Terry was viewing making money while working from home and raising five kids as filled with struggle and had a constant tug of war between the two. Many of us brought up in the U.S. with middle class beliefs see our world through a lens of hard work = money.

What makes up your lens? Did you grow up hearing about how money doesn't grow on trees? Or the people on the other side of town are "filthy rich?" Where are you seeing through your mother's eyes or your grandparents eyes? Through the youth minister's eyes? Your boss's eyes?

How can you become aware of your lens and how you view things?

You can begin by looking around you and at the results you have in your life right now. Are you always in a state of worry? Short on cash? Alone? Bored? Busy? Stressed?

Start becoming aware of your thoughts. More than that, specifically become aware of the questions you ask yourself in your mind and how you answer them. Most of us focus on the same five stories, and repeat them over and over again. Stories of our unfaithful spouse, worry about money or college tuition for kids or making the rent. We may worry about our kids getting along at school or what our busy-body neighbors think if we don't mow our lawn every week.

Our thoughts can be a spinning, never-ending cycle of doom that can be difficult to break out of. As you dream and plot out your map of where you are, where you want to go, and formulate your next step, start to become aware of the automated answers you give to the questions you ask.

For example, "What's my next step?" is a question you may ask. Sometimes questions like this can bring up an automated "I don't know" response. I am going to tell you that yes, you do. You do know. You may have to ask and wait for the answer to be clear, however, you know. This is your life. It's your purpose. In fact, *only you* know the answer to the question, what's your next step. I can guide you and show you options, but ultimately only you are in charge.

Another common response to the question "What's my next step" is to start listing all the reasons we can't do something. Why we shouldn't rather than why we should. "It's irresponsible." "I'm being selfish if I don't put my kids first." "I need to pay off all my debt and have six months living expenses in savings first." "I may get hurt." "She needs to prove herself to me before I give her my heart." The list goes on and on. These automated responses quickly pop up when people are facing a fear; such as being asked to spend money or step into a new relationship!

The "how I can" versus "why I can't lens"

Your outlook is key...

One of the biggest reasons we aren't living our dream lives is because we don't see how we can possibly get from point A to point B. By default we see all the reasons we can't do things, not all the ways we can. Because we can't see how inertia sets in and we simply stand still. Most of us don't have role models to show us the way, and we aren't accustomed to creating opportunity from seemingly nothing.

When you can begin to look at your world through the lens of opportunity and possibility instead of defaulting to the focus of all the reasons why you can't, everything changes. It takes time, patience and persistence to constantly look at everything that happens and every step you take as an opportunity rather than a dead end or a recipe for disaster.

Why do you default to the "why I can't" lens? Part of it may be your upbringing. Part of it may be the people you have surrounded yourself with. Also understand your ego is stepping in, like it is supposed to, and the ego is trying to protect you. Protecting you is the sole purpose of its existence and it knows your buttons and will push all of them with no shame to keep you nice and safe where you are!

Creating the "what I want" lens versus "solving the problem" lens

As we discussed briefly in Chapter 3, we all are groomed from a young age to solve problems rather than create something new. The lens we see our situations through is "this is a problem." What if we approached changing our lives or our businesses or anything we desire from a place of creating—like an artist does with a blank canvas or a writer does with a blank page? Instead of "this is a problem to solve" see the situation as "what do I want to create?"

I invite you to create your Fresh Tracks, not solve the problem of getting from point A to point B. What do you want to create? Your life is a tapestry and you get to design the outcome. How wonderful and powerful and fun that is!

It's up to you to choose to spend your time looking for all the ways the Universe brings you opportunity so you can create your tapestry. Why focus on seeing all the reasons you can't? Why be a victim? Your challenge is to remain open to seeing the opportunity to create your Fresh Tracks rather than solve the problem of fixing your current life.

BECOMING AWARE OF YOUR BELIEFS

What are your core values? What are your beliefs? How do your beliefs affect the lens you view the world through?

Each of us has our own unique set of beliefs that we know to be true. Most of our beliefs were formed based on experiences with our family, our friends, and the community we lived in when we grew up. Amazingly, these beliefs were formed before the age of seven, and are still stored in our subconscious!

Your subconscious mind is a massive storage house of memories. Its function is to store memories so you don't have to keep relearning the same things repeatedly. Our sense of identity and who we become as adults is very much based on the words we've heard, the modeling and major experiences we had before the age of seven. When we are young we are simply learning to navigate our world, and these first experiences form most of what we perceive. The job of the subconscious mind is to, without judgement, play these perceptions out in the circumstances of our life. Creating our perceptions is what our subconscious mind is supposed to do. It does this without conscious thought and, based on our perceptions, navigates our reactions, feelings and emotions in life. It keeps us safe.

We often base our dreams and the actions we take towards achieving them on what we *think* we can do based on our belief system. How high we set our goals, how big we vision, even the greatness of the adventures we set out on are based on what we believe to be possible.

What we don't know is that many of our beliefs are not true. We perceive things based on what we perceived to be true as a child, which may no longer be true for us now.

Let's look at an example. Imagine how a four-year-old views events in her life. Even the most loving of parents can get frustrated with a youngster who spills milk on new carpet and say something that leaves an imprint on an impressionable mind. The tired and busy parents may tell the child how clumsy she is and be incredibly angry and yell in exasperation. That feeling of being clumsy and associating making mistakes with being yelled at or letting down someone she loves may repeat itself in situations as an adult. Unknowingly, beliefs of getting in trouble when making a mistake or fear of letting someone you love down if you do something wrong can sway decision-making as an adult. As a child, you didn't know your parents were tired and stressed from a busy day at work. You didn't know they spent every last penny they had on the new carpet and were trying to sell the house. You were a child and related being clumsy with loss of love.

How can you discover what beliefs you do have? You can start by looking at the results in your life to see what you really believe. This can be different than what your mouth says you believe, so be open! Sometimes we know the "right" thing to say, yet deep down we don't believe it.

Do you experience lack? Worry about things that haven't happened yet? Struggle to maintain healthy relationships? Not follow your passions? Are bored to tears because you play it safe in life?

Here's an example of how this works. If you believe it's hard to make money you will unconsciously look for people and events that support your belief that it's hard to make money. That's the lens you see the world through and that's what you'll see. You will struggle to make money. You'll probably be surrounded by other people who struggle to make money as well.

Conversely, if you believe it's easy to make money, you'll find plentiful opportunity to make money.

Relationships are another great example that you may experience struggle with or see struggle with some of your friends. Some people struggle their entire lives to find love. Others have no problem finding their perfect mate, even if they decide to move on from a relationship, they are able to find love again.

What do you believe to be true about creating your Fresh Tracks?

Start paying attention.

When you start making changes in your life you are going to get some kickback.

As you continue on your path creating Fresh Tracks, what you are doing may seem illogical, even irresponsible to your friends and family because it's new and different to them. And odds are it's something none of them would do. It wasn't the path they chose and they may feel threatened, intimidated, or even angry to see you taking risks and moving forward with your life. It's actually quite common for this to happen.

How can you best handle this?

First, do your best to prepare for it. Keep your dreams close to your chest, be prepared that some may not support you, and go forward anyway.

Stepping past The Edge will change you. It will change you for the better and for the rest of your life. There's no undoing the growth you'll experience. Some of your loved ones may feel resentful of this and not connect with you as intimately because you've changed and they haven't. Give them some space and time to adjust and continue on your journey strong, knowing you trust yourself.

When you do reach The Edge it should be scary as hell! Sometimes this fear is financial, for example leaving your safe, secure corporate job to start your own business is naturally going to bring some fear up. Part of the fear may be because you are breaking family or societal norms by stepping outside of tradition and there is fear of loss or judgement. If you do experience fear, try to recognize the root cause of it. For example, you may worry about being disowned by your family or ridiculed by your sibling for failing. You can rationally decide if that fear justifies the pain of not continuing on your path to cut Fresh Tracks.

Many people sit on the fence before taking their big leap and blame their fear on something outside of themselves, but the truth is that what they are afraid of is trusting themselves. Trusting themselves to do whatever it takes to succeed. Trusting themselves to keep their word to themselves. It's interesting, most of us will keep our word to someone else, but not to ourselves. And what that does is build a center of distrust and fear around committing to ourselves. No one else cares if you keep your word to yourself—in fact most people won't even know if you break your word. It is up to you to keep your word to yourself and strengthen the muscle of truth and integrity with yourself.

Mistakes and failures are eminent. Expect them and make the decision to continue moving in spite of them. Toughen up. Draw that line in the sand and say "Now." Don't get surprised or discouraged or beat yourself up when you don't get what you expected the first or the fifth or the twentieth time. Determination and endurance are character traits that you must embrace to cut Fresh Tracks. Do what you can to keep your spirits up and stay positive. Workshops, positive movies, and like-minded friends can all keep you motivated to continue on.

In-depth training from Kelly on Chapter 4 is available here: http://kellyrobbins.net/tynsadvancedmaterial/

The advanced material will give you access to a training video from Kelly, a recap of the chapter, a top tip from the chapter and a challenge for you!

Work along with the book in the *Trust Your Next Step Workbook* http://kellyrobbins.net/trust-next-step-workbook/

CHAPTER 5

UNDERSTANDING THE STUFF YOU'VE GOT TO WORK WITH

PRINCIPLE IS NOT BOUND BY PRECEDENT

THOMAS TROWARD

Discovering your beliefs, particularly beliefs that don't support you in creating Fresh Tracks, is an important part of changing the results in your life.

In addition to recognizing any hidden, unsupportive beliefs we have, it's just as important we understand what IS possible. What are we capable of, truly, and how much of this do we believe is true? Most of us have false truths we are not aware of that limit what we believe is possible.

When looking at beliefs we must start at the beginning. Where do we come from and what are we made of? First, it's important to understand we all have access to the same tools and come from the same substance. How we use this substance is what varies. In this chapter, we are going to take an in-depth look at what that substance is. I believe having a deep understanding of this is imperative to your success in cutting your own Fresh Tracks.

One of my favorite quotes is by the great teacher Thomas Troward. He said "Principle is not bound by precedent." To me this means that just because I have always gotten a certain result—such as never making more than $2,000 a month in my business—doesn't mean I can't make more than $2,000 a month in my business (precedent). Most of us can easily agree with this. The subtlety in this statement is: what does Principle mean?

Principle is Universal Law, and we all need to know, understand, and master what IS possible. What is Universal Law? What is Principle and where am I following it and not following it?

Universal Laws cross all religions and are spiritual truths by which we all live. They are simply truths.

If you are struggling to create a change in your life, or certain parts of your life are not working, you are struggling because you are not following a Universal Law correctly. If you don't even know what they are it's hard to determine if you are following them correctly!

Universal Laws are spiritual truths, yet, this is not a teaching about religion. Spiritual truths cross all religions. You can practice no religion at all and still understand and utilize the Principles of Universal Law and, most importantly, discover where you are and are not following the Law.

Why are Universal Laws important to know and understand? Because many of our beliefs (both conscious and unconscious) are not in alignment with Universal Law. In fact, some of our beliefs contradict the laws and that is why understanding these may be the most important part of this book!

Be open to the fact that if you are not receiving a result in your life it is because you are not following a Universal Law. Yet you might be doing what YOU KNOW TO BE TRUE. And what you know to be true may be wrong.

Recognize where you have a belief that is not in alignment with a Universal Truth, and then see where this untrue belief is stopping you from creating what you want in life. Following this process is a game changer and can make creating your Fresh Tracks effortless!

There is a book by Raymond Holliwell called *Working with the Law*. It lists 11 truth principles for successful living that are easy to understand and implement. I have based my 12 Universal Laws off his book, with some changes and additions. If you Google Universal Law you will find tons of "Universal Laws" people have put together. I saw a list of 101 once! I don't think that's manageable or realistic and most of them stem from these 12. Take an objective look at this list of 12 and see how they resonate with you. Understand these laws intertwine and there will be some repetition in the explanations. There are subtle differences between each of them and it's important you pay attention to the intent and the nuances between them.

This is a list and a short description of each of the 12 Universal Laws:

LAW #1–THE LAW OF THINKING

Your dominant thoughts are what you manifest. Period. If the majority of your thoughts are negative or filled with worry and doubt, that is what you will experience in life. If the majority of your thoughts are of growth, success and opulence, that is what you will experience in life. Like attracts like. What is in your mind is what takes form in your world. What you think, you are. Do you think you are funny and a great speaker? Then you are. Do you think you are fat, boring and struggle in all your relationships? Then you do.

Imagine your mind is like fertile soil; what you plant will grow. If you plant weeds, they will grow. If you plant flowers, they will grow. The flowers and the weeds represents the growth or the manifestation you are experiencing in life. The thoughts that you think repeatedly are the thoughts that become fixed in your subconscious mind and become true. All of the things you want to change on the outside, the focus needs to start on the inside. You can't think about creating wealth, and then spend your time worrying about the economy and the huge pile of bills you can't make a dent in.

The Law of Thinking involves three phases. The first phase is the thought or idea that comes to you. Let's visualize the idea as a seed. In order for the seed to grow it needs to be planted and cared for in healthy soil. The second phase in the creative process is the soil. The soil is representative of your mind…the beliefs you hold, your attitude and expectations. The seed is planted in the healthy and fertile soil and then we wait for it to take root and grow. We care for the soil by pulling out the weeds and making room for the seed we planted to take root and grow. The third phase is the manifestation—this manifestation is what you create in this world. The new shoes, the healthy relationships, love, abundance, joy, etc.

In our example today we plant a rose seed and grow a rose. There is no way we will plant a rose seed and grow a sunflower or an oak tree. If you are growing oak trees and frustrated because you are trying to grow roses, take a look at the seeds you are planting!

You can take a look at your life and see what seeds you are planting. What are you experiencing? What are you continuously thinking about? This Law states your dominant thoughts, not your "one time I tried really hard" thoughts, are what you bring to fruition. What different seeds will you need to plant to cut your Fresh Tracks?

As long as you allow things to seem real to you, you are putting your energy into them and keeping them alive. This includes lack of anything, debt, poor health, no opportunity, relationships, etc.

How to use the Law of Thinking: Becoming aware of thought patterns and changing thought patterns that don't support the direction you choose to go is not only possible, but mandatory to mastering this law.

Pick an area of your life you would like to improve. For example, your relationship with your partner.

1. Make a list of positive things about your partner. What do you admire? Read the list before bed and each morning upon awakening at a minimum.

2. Set a timer for every 30 minutes or an hour and write down a positive trait of your partner.

3. Flip the switch. Catch yourself complaining or focusing on negative thoughts. Becoming aware of them and the stories you are stuck on is a first step. Changing them to positive thoughts and getting untangled from the negatives stories is the second step.

Changing your continuous thought patterns takes focus, yet change can happen incredibly quickly if you are determined and disciplined in catching and changing the focus of your thoughts from where they have been to where you want them to go. I recommend you focus on one thing at a time and go full force paying attention to your thinking patterns and changing them.

Law # 2–The Law of Supply

There is an unlimited supply of everything good you can imagine. AND, you are entitled to a never-ending supply of anything you desire or need. Always. The secret to this law lies in your consciousness and what you believe to be true.

Many of us spend our time worrying about where the money or the relationship (or whatever) will come from. What if you just knew it would come and didn't worry about how or where it came from? There is more than enough supply of money, time, good health, love to give, mountains to climb, people to hug, wines to taste.

The thing is we don't believe that. In fact it's not what we see to be true. Most of us see and hear about limits and lack rather than abundance and supply.

The truth is limits only come from the belief in limits itself. There is no cap on how much love you can receive. Just as there is no cap on how much wealth you can accumulate in a day. There is no such thing as lack of opportunity—there is a never-ending supply of opportunity! If you know it and expect it.

The extent that you are able to embrace the fact that there is unlimited supply is the extent that you are able to receive it. Imagine how different it is to manifest what you want in this way!

Nature is a terrific example of the Law of Supply. Flowers don't struggle and worry if there is enough air, enough fertile soil, enough water, or if the flower next to them is a prettier color. They simply seek out what they need and flourish. Birds and other animals are always working to build their nests and find food, yet they never worry. They simply get busy doing what they need to do, fully expecting to find what they need.

Supply always comes on the heels of demand, states Robert Collier, the metaphysical teacher and author of *The Secret of the Ages*. That means you need to ask for what you want and seek it out, not wait for it to land in your lap! *Your job is to command and lead*, not cringe when it comes to staking your claim and creating what you want in life.

An interesting fact: Nature never builds downhill, always up. So know as one desire is realized, another larger desire will develop. This is an amazing fact because the moguls on the ski mountain crawl up the mountain throughout the ski season! They aren't made by the snow falling down on top of itself, which is what you might assume. They crawl uphill, even though the skiers and snow move downhill. Your dreams work this way too—you need to reach and stretch yourself up to the next level and the supply will be available to you. And so will your dreams and greater experiences in life if you understand there is a never-ending supply.

How to use the Law of Supply: Actively look for the opportunity for what you want, knowing that it is there. Look for it in a curious way rather than a problem solving way. Be playful and curious to discover how fun it is to find where your opportunity is appearing for you right now! Your next step may appear in a song, comments someone makes, a child's sing-song jabbering. Be open and curious, KNOWING what you seek will appear. Your job is to see it.

Be clear on what you want, knowing it will appear, and then start moving towards making it a reality—fully expecting it to. Because supply is limitless.

Law #3–Law of Attraction

The basic premise of the Law of Attraction is that like creates like.

At first glance the Law of Attraction is similar to the Law of Thinking. Thoughts = things. That is true, but this law is slightly different in that it's focus is on the energy of you and how you vibrate, which often boils down to what you predominately think about. While vibration is a common word folks use to describe the Law of Attraction, I believe resonance describes it better. Let's take a deeper look at resonance:

Have you ever played with a tuning fork? If you tap it, it will resonate at its natural frequency of 256 Hz. If there are any other tuning forks in the area they will begin resonating at the exact same frequency without being tapped. It's called resonance—when one object vibrating at the same natural frequency of a second object forces that second object into vibrational motion. This is what the Law of Attraction is in its most basic form. Our bodies naturally vibrate, just like everything else in the Universe. How we think, how we are being, effects the frequency at which our bodies vibrate.

Everything is energy and energy is always moving. Energy cannot stop moving and cannot disappear, it can only change forms. Your job is to raise your natural frequency to what you want to attract. Your thoughts play a tremendous role in the rate your body is vibrating. For example, lack has a lower frequency than abundance. Worry has a lower vibrational state than peace.

Let's use the example of your interest in making more money and the Law of Attraction. If you are working 80 hours a week making $25 an hour, there is no additional time in the day for you to make more money doing what you currently do. Being interested in making more money is not enough to kick this law into gear, but it is where we start! Which leads us to the second facet of the Law of Attraction.

The second facet is where you place your attention. In our money example you would start resonating to more money (abundance) by focusing on ways that allow you to charge more, expand your offerings, or do something completely different. As a freelance copywriter I ran out of time in the day to work more hours, and charging an hourly rate I was stuck at a maximum income. I began putting my attention on how to make money that was not related to specific copywriting projects by the hour. I began studying and buying online trainings and courses to learn more about the information marketing industry. I started focusing my attention on what I wanted to do next to make more money in less time. I expanded my offerings and put my attention on new ways to make money given a new criteria (time ≠ money).

Giving your area of interest attention means doing something to bring it to fruition. You cannot meditate your way through life and attract your desires! Start taking action, moving towards your goal or desire. I started creating and selling training products online, which eventually led to The Copywriting Institute. As I gave attention to my goals and studied and got involved in growing in this way, I began to resonate with making money in this way and was able to build a successful online business.

Expectation is the final of the three facets of the Law of Attraction. This means that you fully expect to achieve positive results, with intensity and anticipation. If you step into anything expecting poor results, that's what you'll get (because that is where you are resonating) and at the same time you will get the good you desire if you expect to get it (because that is where you are resonating).

I believe changing your natural resonance or vibration requires you to not only be aware of and change your thoughts, but also take action towards physically creating the change. That's how the Fresh Tracks are created. Let's look at one more example using the Law of Attraction to have positive, healthy friendships.

Interest—you realize you either don't like your friends, you don't have any friends, or you would like to consciously push yourself to find new friends who are healthier or more like-minded. You find that you are avoiding the friends you do have and spend most of your time at home alone, watching television. Or you go to the gym and work out after work but don't talk to anyone there.

Putting your attention on making new friends may start with you taking action towards attracting fun and healthy friendships. This requires you to get out and do something to meet them—not veg out on the couch each evening! Or setting a goal for yourself that you will strike up one conversation each time you go to the gym. That's the action or attention required, along with putting your thoughts and focus on attracting new friendships.

The third aspect to changing your friend group is actually expecting that you can and will accomplish this goal. You can expect that you will accomplish it easily or you can expect that it will be difficult—again that's up to you. You won't make positive friendships sitting on your couch watching television every day. You have to get out and meet people, knowing and expecting that you will make some new friends.

How to use the Law of Attraction: Thoughts create things— again this law requires you to be conscious of your thoughts. Using the Law of Attraction in your life requires you to be clear on what it is you want to create, focus your attention on creating more of that, and then watch for and expect it to happen. Figure out what you really want. Understand why you want it—what feelings are attached to it? Is there anything else that gives you the same feeling as achieving your goal? What can you compare the feeling with? Do the things that give you the same feelings and hold that state for as long as possible, as frequently as possible. For example, I remember the surprise and joy I experienced the first time I sold a product online while I was sleeping. I was ecstatic and hooting and hollering and jumping for joy when I received the notification email of the sale! My dog and my baby daughter joined in the celebration it was so fantastic. I remember that feeling and do my best to bring it up whenever I create and launch a new product.

Interest, attention, and expectation are the three facets to using this law effectively. If you desire more money or better friendships, it's up to you to do things that get you excited and will lead you down a path to achieving more money or better friendships.

Law #4–Law of Giving and Receiving

This law is all about circulation. Circulating love, joy, abundance—the basic idea is anything you want you must first circulate yourself. Circulation can be in the form of compliments, well wishes, love, appreciation, money, time, anything and everything you can think of. Giving and receiving go hand in hand and both are required for you to enjoy this law to the fullest.

You are continually drawing into life what you give and what you expect to receive. Keep in mind giving and receiving are mutually exclusive in that giving to get breaks the spirit or the intention of the law. You give because you can and you do so knowing that everything you give will come back to you tenfold. You must also have a willingness to give what you want more of. Giving and receiving are different aspects of the universal flow of energy; they are two polarities of the same frequency spectrum of abundance.

Let us start with a deeper look at giving…

Give your substance (your time, your money, your love and attention) where it will do the most good—not to people who don't appreciate it, don't want it, or are lazy. Nature doesn't support a parasite or a slouch and neither should you. Be smart about your giving and don't give haphazardly or foolishly, give strategically and carefully. It is consistency in giving and not the size of the giving that matters most. It is better to give frequently in small amounts than less frequently in large amounts. Correct giving must be a circulation and not just an outflow. When you give, you need to receive something in return in order to enable yourself to give more. You may receive from a completely different person, so don't give expecting it to come back immediately in exactly the same form. Another tip to using this law to its fullest is to always give away what you want. If you want love, give love. If you want knowledge, give knowledge.

Now let's take a look at receiving...

Many people aren't aware that they aren't open to receiving. You must be open to receiving and be fully expecting you will get what you ask for—and it often comes in ways you don't expect. Receiving is not getting. Receiving is about allowing something to come to you.

Notice how you respond to compliments, particularly when they are sincere. Do you quickly discount it, deny it or ignore it? Learn to accept yourself so you can look the person complimenting you in the eye and say "Thank you." Accept something good when it is offered to you. When you refuse a gift from someone, you are not only blocking the flow of abundance in your life, but you are blocking it in theirs as well.

How to use the Law of Giving and Receiving: An example is wishing for new clothes and taking the time to clean out your closet. Expecting to receive a new wardrobe, cleaning out your closet to make room for your new clothes before they have arrived is a great way to be open to receiving them. Nature abhors a vacuum—rest assured that closet won't stay empty for long! Just give your old clothes away—don't be a miser and store them or hoard them. This law thrives on flow and circulation.

LAW #5–LAW OF GRATITUDE

What you are grateful for you will see more of. The key to this law is to praise and appreciate what you want to see more of in your life. Don't put your focus on praising what has happened in the past (for example a profitable quarter), but praise the future of what is to come. Praise is complementary to faith and involves you knowing that what you expect to happen will. More love, more health, more money.

When you hold the space of gratitude, even for the smallest things, it will bring you more of that. The predominant way of being when you are using this law is to praise from your heart with meaning, not intellectually from your head and mouth, which is simply going through the motions of gratitude. It's more than what words you say it's how you feel as you are saying it. Gratitude is both a feeling and an attitude, and is expressed by being thankful and appreciative. You have to mean it!

The truth is you can't gain more of anything if you fail to appreciate what you already have. Lack of gratitude closes you off from receiving and complaining brings you more of what you don't want. This law is also called the Law of Increase—whatever you praise you will see an increase in. When you praise you are raising the vibration of you, what you see, and how you react.

The opposite of praise and gratitude is condemnation and complaining. Do you complain about how broke you are? The economy? Your job? Your partner? When you do this you are increasing what you don't want because that is what you are focusing on!

Have you ever worked hard to make a new meal or complete a new project at work and someone comes up and tells you how terrible it is? How did you feel afterwards? Did you want to quit? Not try hard anymore? Move on to something else? Give up? This is the Law of Gratitude in reverse. The more you praise what you are doing, who you are surrounding yourself with, the more you are going to succeed. Gratitude changes how you see things and is an incredibly important trait when cutting Fresh Tracks. It changes your entire outlook on life. In order to praise someone you have to be looking for something good to say—which may be different than your default of noticing what's wrong in a situation.

If you want to receive good things you also have to be open to receiving. Praise what you've got, and share it. Willingly give it, graciously receive it, and praise it.

How to use the Law of Gratitude:

1. Notice if you are noticing everything wrong in situations or if you notice everything right. At work. With your kids. With your partner. Gratitude is a choice. Learn to have gratitude for the small, everyday things in life and not just the big things like the promotion, the new house, etc.

2. You can start a gratitude journal and write down 5 or 25 things you are grateful for every day. This exercise is to bring awareness to positive things in lieu of negative. If you choose a high number and push yourself you will force yourself to pay attention throughout the day rather than scramble around at night!

3. Write a letter to someone you are grateful for. Keep it or give it to them, the exercise is about recognizing you are grateful for them.

Law #6–The Law of Cause and Effect

Every action has a reaction or consequence. The Law of Cause and Effect states that whatever you put out today is what's going to come back to you. In other words, what you reap is what you sow.

Understand that life is not a random set of occurrences, but is a predictable and repeatable formula of conscious free choice. Everything that you currently have in your life is an effect that is the result of a specific cause. Life isn't built by accidents, luck or fate—we have free choice. Because nothing happens by accident or luck, we have to conclude that we are the cause. We are responsible for the results or effects we have in our lives, good or bad.

This law states that the universe is always in motion and progresses from a chain of events.

The Law of Cause and Effect is actually considered the foundation of Buddhism, which calls it the Law of Karma. Ralph Waldo Emerson famously called this law the "law of laws." The Law of Cause and Effect is also known as Newton's third law, defined by the physicist Isaac Newton, "For every action there is an equal and opposite reaction." This applies to our physical realities as well as our spiritual, mental and emotional selves.

If you are not happy with the effects you have created in your life then you must change the causes that created them. The causes are the decisions we make and the actions we take every day. Every decision we make and every action we take, no matter how big or small, set events into motion that create specific and predictable effects we are now experiencing.

In order to consciously create your Fresh Tracks you need to be able to back up what actions, what feelings, and what behaviors will cause you to create from that place. We are not accustomed to looking at our life in this way and it can take practice.

If you can define an effect that you want, you can trace it back to a cause and repeat it. You can do this by following the tracks of successful people. Nature is neutral. It doesn't care who is doing it, it only cares that you follow its laws.

The challenge in this is that we each start from a different place, yet have access to the exact same laws to work with. We are born with a unique and specific set of characteristics, personality and temperament. Our unique past, our parents and cultural influences, our present actions, mental attitude, intellect, physical body, and moral character makes us each different. We each have to back into our cause from a different place. We can create by learning and following what others have done, yet our journey back to our original cause will be different because we are different. It's necessary to make different, individual adjustments to follow the law correctly. This is why cookie-cutter formulas and how-to kits don't always work. My journey is not the same as yours because my starting point is different than yours.

How to use the Law of Cause and Effect:

1. Start by becoming aware of something in your life you are not happy with, an effect. The truth is you can just as easily look at something in your life you are ecstatic about as something you are unhappy with because it's the same law. The law works the same regardless of your judgement of the outcome!

2. Ask why you have this outcome or effect. Trace it back to the core cause or the root cause—which will be use or misuse of a Universal Principle. It is not always easy to track all the way back to the cause because most of us have not done it before and it is a new skill. It can be helpful to have an experienced coach working with you to help guide you. Generally, keep asking "why" until you have to think about your answers. Ask until the default answers you are accustomed to using are no longer valid—get to where you have to think! Trace it back until you reach a feeling of love, security or self-esteem. The causes are often hidden, yet in plain sight. The key is in asking the right questions—which are not always outcome based.

3. Be conscious of the choices you make in each moment. Being present today is the best way to create the effects you want in life tomorrow.

Law #7–Law of Compensation

When you improve yourself, you will attract better things and will be given greater things to do. If you want to make more you need to give more and grow more so you can receive more. The crux of the Law of Compensation is there are natural consequences to your actions and you reap what you sow proportionately. Every time we choose an action we choose a consequence to that action.

Ralph Waldo Emerson says in his Law of Compensation essay, "Every act rewards itself." When you do your tasks the best you can, you bring out the best in yourself. You grow and become more capable. When you become too large for your present place you then draw something larger to you, which may be more money, more love, more confidence, etc. The Law doesn't limit itself to money as compensation. Compensation for one act may come in many different forms and from many different sources. Some of it may seem strange and unexpected—so it's important you be open to seeing and receiving the compensation from wherever it appears.

What's important to know about this Law is that you cannot draw something bigger to yourself until you first become larger. It is your responsibility to become larger and continue to grow, which you do when you cut Fresh Tracks. No one will do this for you and it requires you to be self-motivated, maintain a sense of urgency, and take repeated action. Use the Law of Cause and Effect and implement "causes" in your life that will lead to the effect you seek.

Napoleon Hill, author of the classic book *Think and Grow Rich*, interviewed Andrew Carnegie about why some people, even hard workers, are stuck making a "daily wage." Carnegie said it is because "98 out of 100 of them have no definite plan or purpose greater than a daily wage. Therefore, no matter how hard they work or how much they do, or how well they do it, the wheel of fortune will turn on past them without providing them more than a bare living—because they neither expect nor demand more." He then goes to share how he demands riches in definite terms, has a definite plan for acquiring riches, and is engaged in carrying out that plan and is giving an equivalent of useful service equal to the value of the riches he demands.

Understand it is the order of nature to grow, and just as crabs molt and shed their outer shell, we must do the same as we grow. Yet we often resist this personal expansion. We hang on to old friends, jobs we don't like, beliefs that are no longer true for us, and even our faith that no longer serves us in our new position. Just like the crab sheds it's shell and builds itself a new house when it outgrows it, so must we. We resist parting with old friends. We idealize the old times, the old us, not believing we can recreate the wonderfulness of yesterday. When we do this we don't grow, in fact we impair the Law of Compensation. You can't make more if you don't become more. You can't become more if you are hanging on tightly to the old.

How to use the Law of Compensation: Increase your value, give more than you get. Do more than you are paid for. Understand how cause and effect works and implement the causes in your life that will lead to the effects you desire. Remind yourself that your rewards are always in direct proportion to the value of the contribution you gave yesterday.

———

Law #8–Law of Non-Resistance

Whatever you resist persists. When negative events happen in our lives it's often an instinct to fight it. To resist what we don't want. Nonresistance is the ability to not be affected by something, especially something negative.

How can you not let negative things affect you and what does that have to do with creating Fresh Tracks?

By working towards and focusing on what you do want, by searching for opportunities to continuously move where you choose to rather than focusing on what's coming up that you don't want or that seems to be blocking you, you stay in a flow of harmony and power. This law teaches that you don't work to solve or fix what you don't want, but keep your eye on where you do want to go. Whenever you resist a problem you are giving more power to it and you bring more of it to fruition.

The way the law works is it sees "attention" as "intention," so by focusing your attention on what you do want you are staying true to the intention of what you are creating. Resistance is a normal thing when you are growing and expanding, and it is likely to rear its ugly head as you cut Fresh Tracks—the key is to not react, but respond. When you react you are following a habit, when you respond you have to think.

Let's say you feel you don't have enough money. You have debt. Don't work to solve the problem of debt—work towards building prosperity. This law doesn't ask you to work against what you don't want, but to work with and towards what you do want. How do you do this? Do not give your time, energy or thoughts to the opposite of what you want (the problem). When there is no emotional response to an inharmonious situation, it fades away forever. It removes itself from your pathway. In the building prosperity example, imagine that an unexpected bill pops up. Using the Law of Nonresistance you deal with the new bill without getting all charged up and continue on with your focus on building prosperity.

Water and air are both terrific examples of nonresistance. Air and water do not stop at every wall they meet, and they don't try to go through it. They don't put up a fight when something gets in the way of where they are trying to go. They get where they want to go by offering no resistance—if something gets in their path they nonjudgmentally take a different route. They are committed to their direction and flexible in how they get there. Think of how water runs downhill. It goes around or over rocks, bushes, even houses if need be.

When we choose not to fight something negative that comes into our lives, the energy dissipates because there is no negative energy to get the flame started.

Let's examine another example of how to use the Law of Nonresistance. Let's say you would like a new car because your car is older and the transmission may go out soon. Rather than focusing on your piece of crap car and how ugly it is and dreading getting in it each day, focus your thoughts on how nice it feels getting into your new car. What color is best? What type of car will you get? How will it feel driving it? How cool will you be zipping down the street in it? What will all your friends think? Do you see the difference in focus?

How to work with the Law of Non-Resistance: When you catch yourself experiencing resistance, ask yourself these questions:

1. Can I accept this person or situation exactly as it is?

2. Can I forgive this person or situation for not being what I wanted it to be? Can I forgive myself for wanting this person or situation to be something different?

3. Why am I resisting this? Is it true right now?

4. Will this reason for resisting be true forever?

These four questions are designed to help you take a step back from the situation and view the event you are resisting from a higher perspective. To take the charge or energy off it immediately so you can choose to respond rather than react. Changing a behavior such as resistance can take repeated focus and discipline. Once you answer the questions and have taken the charge off a little bit, you may set a timer to remind yourself to bring your focus back to nonresistance. I find every 30 minutes or an hour is a good amount of time—there are several free apps you can get on your phone as a friendly reminder to focus and be non-resistant during a challenging time.

LAW # 9–LAW OF FORGIVENESS

Forgiveness is about recognizing and honoring why an action that hurt you occurred, and then letting it go. When you forgive, you are letting go of being a victim, blaming others, holding resentments and carrying judgements against others. Forgiveness means to let go of or abandon completely. Forgiveness does not mean forgetting, nor does it mean condoning or excusing offenses.

Forgiving is releasing the need to condemn or punish someone and letting go of any feelings you have of being a victim. I love this quote by Lewis B. Smedes, "To forgive is to set a prisoner free and discover that the prisoner was you." Wanting to assert your rightness or your victimhood is a way of holding power over another. In truth, when we forgive, we are repairing where we have made mistakes or wronged others.

When you condemn, either yourself or another, it takes up negative space in your mind. Space that is better filled with thoughts of abundance, love and other healthy thoughts. It's a good practice to form the habit of not holding on to anything that makes you feel bad.

Negative feelings, thoughts, words and behaviors affect our mental and physical health, our self-esteem and our sense of self-worth. Forgiveness is not something we do for another person, it's something we do for ourselves. By refusing to forgive, we hang on to feelings of blame, judgment, guilt, resentments, hurts and do not make room for the positive emotions and feelings we need to cut Fresh Tracks.

Understand forgiveness is an act of will. You have to make yourself do it because it sets you free.

How to use the Law of Forgiveness: There are several ways to forgive. Try out different methods to find what works best for you. Each situation is also different, so what works in one situation may not work in another. Here are a few methods that have worked for me:

1. Create a forgiveness inventory. Make a list of every event that has ever happened to you and every event where you feel you have done something to someone. What role did you play in the event? Whom do you need to forgive? You can make a list of each person you would like to forgive and begin forgiving both them and yourself for each instance. Look back through your childhood, teen years, school, and work life through now. Parents, friends, family members, teachers, work colleagues, etc.

2. It can help to write letters to each person you want to forgive and ceremoniously shred them or burn them.

3. Sharing your stories out loud with someone you trust, or apologizing and taking steps to mend or heal the relationship goes a long way in the forgiveness process.

4. Forgive the person you choose to forgive by writing, "I Kelly, forgive Joey, completely." Write this statement 70 times a day for seven days. You can break it into 35 statements in the morning and 35 in the evening. After that is complete add on seven days of "I, Kelly, forgive myself completely" 70 times a day, with the intention that your role in the relationship needs forgiving too. It's incredibly important that as you do the writing you don't rush it simply to get it done, but feel the emotions of what it brings up and let it out.

Cry. Get angry. Feel what you need to feel and release it, don't hold it in. I bet you'll find by the end of the fourteen days there isn't much emotion coming up around the event.

5. Spend time each night before you go to bed doing a forgiveness checklist of your day. Is there anyone you have wronged today or anyone you judged? Take the time to examine the situation, the role you played in it, and forgive them.

Forgiveness work is ongoing work and not something you jam out one day and then you are suddenly and miraculously free of grudges! Digging deep into releasing pent-up stories and emotions is a decision that requires follow-through and commitment. Spending time each day focusing on who and what in your life needs forgiving can take a few years if you dig deep and reflect over the different people you've encountered throughout your lifetime. While time-consuming, forgiving others on a deep level changes who YOU are on a deep level. Give yourself the gift of time, and grace yourself with some honest introspection as you begin to heal through forgiving.

Law #10–Law of Sacrifice

To have something of greater value in your life you must be willing to give up something of lesser value. This law tells us that to have something new in your life, you will always have to give something away. Sacrifice does not mean giving up something for nothing, it means giving up something for something better.

It's easy to struggle with this law because society tells us we don't need to sacrifice to obtain things. "Lose weight and keep eating your favorite foods," "get rich in four hours a week," and "buy now, pay later" are a small sampling of what we are exposed to each day.

There is a spiritual maturity that happens when you grow though utilizing this law, and this maturity has to happen for you to keep what you want. A great example of people not maturing and losing what they gain is the majority of lottery winners—they lose all their money within the first five years. Why? Because they have not built up the spiritual maturity to manage that much money. Sacrificing not only helps get you to where you want to go, but builds the maturity and muscles needed to handle the life you build. To reach your goals you have to move forward, which means leaving some things behind along the way. If you try to get where you are going without sacrificing, you end up holding everything and become stuck.

The parent gives up more freedom to enjoy something they feel has greater value, their child. The famous actor gives up their privacy for fame and fortune. The athlete gives up time with their friends and family to hone their talent. The award-winning body builder gives up sweets to enjoy zero percent body fat.

Where people often struggle with the Law of Sacrifice is letting go of actions or behaviors before the new arrives. The key to this law is you "make space" for what you want to create. What makes most of us comfortable is that we want the new first and then we are willing to let go of the old. In the journey towards a toned and slim body I sacrifice time watching television and reading books after work for time at the gym. I also sacrifice my delicious, daily 300-calorie Starbucks drink for a zero-calorie coffee. It takes time for me to enjoy my slim and toned beach body—I have to make the sacrifice first to get there.

How to use the Law of Sacrifice: The law of sacrifice operates at our current value system. If you wonder why you lack the discipline to achieve a certain goal, it is because deep down you don't value that goal as much as you think you do. You value the pizza and beer for dinner rather than the toned body. Not sure what you are valuing that is preventing you from achieving your goal?

Here are a few questions you can ask yourself if you are struggling with the Law of Sacrifice.

1. What should you stop doing?
2. What should you keep doing?
3. What should you start doing?

We will discuss how to change habits in-depth a little later on. The key point for right now to creating change is understanding why you are struggling to stick with your decision to obtain a specific goal. The awareness allows you to be conscious of what you are prioritizing in your life and why. Just because you say you value something doesn't mean you do—your words may not have your true values behind them. They are empty words. Coming to a true understanding of your actual values and what sacrifices need to be made to change can be an empowering way to develop the maturity to grow into your actual goals.

Law #11–Law of Obedience

Be confident in knowing there are no mistakes—ever. The Law is an obedient, blind force, like electricity, and unless we misuse it, works unconditionally. Understand the Law is absolute and is completely impersonal in its actions. If you plant a rose seed, nature does not produce an apple tree, it produces a rose. Nature does not produce an apple tree from a rose seed if the ground is very dry, or it is having a bad day or if we try really hard to wish it into an apple tree because we are hungry for apples. Because the Law is obedient and absolute, a rose seed will always produce a rose bush no matter what.

The truth is, no one would ever expect otherwise because we understand how nature works. We understand the laws of nature. Of course, once the seed is planted it needs adequate water, sunlight and the right temperature to grow. Planting the seed alone is not enough. The Law of Obedience will not allow anything other than a rose to come from a rose seed.

Yet, we don't expect or understand that our actions follow the same set of rules nature provides unconditionally. As human beings we must also learn to use nature's forces in accordance with her laws. Which is exactly why it's so important to understand these laws and what you have to work with. Most of us are going through life with absolutely no idea there are laws at work and are frustrated and beating ourselves up because we think we are planting seeds of abundance and we keep getting bigger bills and more debt.

Recall the Principle of Cause and Effect—that for every action there is a reaction or consequence. The Law is a mechanical force—

it is automatic. Electricity can be used by anyone, no matter if they are Jewish or Catholic, Asian or American. Electricity being a natural law, it can be used by anyone and works anywhere and everywhere. The Law is absolute and we can trust its impersonal action implicitly. Like electricity, Law has no power to reason deductively. Your conscious thought has power, the Law has to obey our thoughts, it knows nothing but to obey; it has no will of its own. This is the Law of Obedience.

The Law of Obedience works the same way for humans as it does for nature, we just have our minds that get in our way and talk us into planting the wrong seeds or not nurturing the seeds once they are planted!

If you plant seeds of worry and despair you will receive exactly what you plant: worry and despair. The Law is absolute in that what seeds you plant is what you will grow. The most important thing you can do to flourish and grow is understand how Universal Law works (which means understanding these Universal Principles!) and start following them to the best of your ability.

When you examine obedience, understand it is not about being subservient to others. It's about having a complete understanding of what tools you have to work with and that using them correctly is the only way you will get the results you seek. It's interesting that the definition of obey is "to behave in accordance to a general principle, natural law, etc."

If you don't understand the Laws you can't be obedient to them. You will violate them all the time because you are programmed to follow man's law and not Universal Principles. It's your job to learn and to follow universal laws, not earthly laws.

A perfect example of man-made laws versus Universal Laws are the examples we shared when discussing the Law of Sacrifice. Such as "Lose weight and never be hungry again" and "Get rock hard abs in 15 minutes a day." These are not Universal Laws but are messages we are exposed to repeatedly each day.

How to use the Law of Obedience: You don't see trees or flowers struggling to grow and flourish, and we don't need to either. Does it feel like you are constantly struggling and flailing in your endeavors? It's because we let our minds take over and we compare ourselves to others and overthink "how" to make things manifest. Nature is a great demonstration of the Law of Obedience because it can't overthink things like we do!

If two roses are planted next to each other, one doesn't compare itself to the other, get jealous because it's a red rose and it wants to be yellow and then decide to not grow. Both roses flourish and grow and become the most beautiful rose they can be. They do what they do—grow. And you can and should do the same.

Focus on yourself, what you know to be true about the Laws, and know the process for creating your Fresh Tracks. Study these Laws and understand them. The Laws are very precise, if you are not experiencing the results you desire, where are you out of alignment with the Law? Take a specific situation you are struggling with and go back through each of the Laws. Where are you out of alignment? If you can't tell, get help. Ask someone you trust, hire a coach, be open to seeing the truth.

LAW #12–LAW OF SUCCESS

Every one of us is designed to succeed because the Universe is conspiring in our favor. Always. Understanding, knowing, and expecting this truth in every act you make, every step you take, is imperative to your knowing and realizing success.

What is success, really, and how is it that you are designed to succeed? Success is, simply put, the accomplishment of an aim or purpose. You are made for progress and growth because it is the nature of human beings to grow and expand. If you are not growing you are dying. Advancement in all things is your overall purpose in life, and knowing this is imperative to your achieving it. Because you have to expect success to get it!

How is the Universe conspiring in your favor? Doesn't that statement alone sound so juicy and wonderful? First of all, realize you were born with all the resources you need to achieve success and it is impossible for those resources to be depleted. Once you declare what you intend to create, such as your Fresh Tracks, everything you need starts coming to you. However, sometimes what we need seems wrong or bad to us in the moment and we don't recognize it as the gift it is! How many times in your life has something "bad" happened and you later looked back and saw why it needed to happen for you to get where you are today?

How would you live your life differently if you knew you were guaranteed success? And if you knew without question there was a limitless supply of everything you needed—that success is inherent? When I say inherent, I mean it is your birthright. This Law asks you to more than expect, it asks that you *demand* success.

Infinite resources are at your disposal and you always know the right action to take. Success is yours when you deal with absoluteness and have that attitude. The idea of a successful life will bring you success. It's up to you to consciously train yourself to conceive of yourself as a success. No one else can do that for you.

Napoleon Hill has famously written about the Law of Success in his classic book *Think and Grow Rich*. He tells us we were made to evolve and expand and enjoy endless growth and development.

If you can hold the belief that the Universe is conspiring in your favor, and if you look at life through that lens, you will achieve success. You will cut your Fresh Tracks. It is guaranteed. Recognize the advancement of all things is this Law's function. By learning to work with the Law in building the intention of success for yourself, you can develop into a greater and greater success and continue to evolve and thrive.

How to use the Law of Success:

Imagine how differently you would go through life if you KNEW you would be successful at whatever endeavor you take on. Mastering this Law requires just that. Let's start by first recognizing when and where we do or do not expect success. What is your success IQ?

> ► Start by paying attention to how you expect events, projects and other endeavors to turn out. Do you expect success? Do you expect failure? Do you do things just to get them done? Are you going through the motions or are you present and engaged with each activity?

▶ Consciously choose the successful outcome you desire and hold it top of mind as often as possible. Set a timer on your phone that goes off every hour or every 30 minutes, often enough to bring your success thoughts top of mind and hold them there.

▶ Create a success mantra and repeat it throughout the day. For example, you may have a dream of writing an article you would like published in a specific magazine. As you are writing it, keep the feeling of seeing it in publication. Write *knowing* it will be published.

The Law of Success is tied closely to faith for me. Your outcomes will change almost instantly if you can catch yourself not expecting success or not fully engaging in activities you are doing. Pay attention, flip the switch in your mind from expected failure to expected success, and begin expecting—no, *demanding*—you receive what you ask for.

Your job, starting right now, is to learn what the Universal Laws are and how they are used in life and business. Study them. Practice them. Watch how others use them, both successfully and unsuccessfully. In which areas of your life are you using them correctly? Where do you need to adjust? Play and have fun with it. Understanding and using these laws correctly is imperative to cutting your Fresh Tracks.

In-depth training from Kelly on Chapter 5 is available here: http://kellyrobbins.net/tynsadvancedmaterial/

The advanced material will give you access to a training video from Kelly, a recap of the chapter, a top tip from the chapter and a challenge for you!

Work along with the book in the *Trust Your Next Step Workbook* http://kellyrobbins.net/trust-next-step-workbook/

CHAPTER 6

EXPECT TO FALL AND GET WET: YOU WILL FAIL

I'VE MISSED MORE THAN 9000 SHOTS IN MY CAREER. I'VE LOST AL-MOST 300 GAMES. TWENTY-SIX TIMES I'VE BEEN TRUSTED TO TAKE THE GAME WINNING SHOT AND MISSED. I'VE FAILED OVER AND OVER AND OVER AGAIN IN MY LIFE. AND THAT IS WHY I SUCCEED."

MICHAEL JORDAN

EXPECT TO FAIL AND QUIT BEATING YOURSELF UP ABOUT IT!

There's a saying in skiing that if you don't fall you're not pushing yourself, which my dad annoyingly repeated to me over and over again as a kid on the ski slopes of Colorado. And not only did he expect me to fall, he made me get up by myself. It can be difficult to stand up after a fall on the snowy mountain. He would walk up the mountain on his skis (which is a lot of work!), stand right next to me and tell me what to do; how to untangle my legs, put my skis back on while standing sideways on the mountain, un-fog my wet goggles so I could see. He never offered a hand or rescued me quickly.

I was miserable.

Now, as a mother, I can see how patient he actually was, waiting for my wailing tears to stop and discouraging me from sliding down the mountain on my butt. Instead, he encouraged me to embrace my fear even after the crash. He wanted me to be confident in myself so I KNEW I was strong enough to get out of any situation.

Through my tears and grumbling with each fall, my dad taught me an important lesson—falling is OK. It is, in fact, expected if you want to get better. What was also expected was that I pick myself back up, don't rely on anyone else to bail me out, get on my way back down the mountain and not catch a ride on a snowmobile (which I only did once when I tried snowboarding).

If you're not falling you're not pushing yourself is an important lesson for all entrepreneurs and for anyone who is cutting Fresh Tracks. You will fall. You will fail. It is expected and in fact it's a good thing because if you aren't falling you aren't growing. If you aren't falling you aren't pushing yourself and your goals are probably not stretching you enough. Let's also recognize right from the beginning that "failing" is a judgment. It is an opinion. We are discussing failure as a judgement because most of us judge ourselves quite harshly.

I challenge you to look at your "failure" as simply a result. It may be the 100th way you've discovered to not accomplish your goal, but it's still a result. As you look at your results objectively, also recognize that there's one more thing you need to do. The last lesson…it's up to you to pick yourself back up.

WHY TRUSTING YOURSELF IS SO IMPORTANT.

Failure is a part of your growth and is a necessary and unavoidable part of the Fresh Tracks process. As humans it's natural to want to avoid the pain and fear involved in falling. We hide our failures from others in shame, and it's not usually talked about so we don't see how others are falling along their way too. We see the success of those we admire, but not the long, painful journey they endured to get there. We try at all costs to master things without experiencing the emotional roller coaster that goes along with mastery.

We can intellectualize failing and understand that it's going to happen, but when it *actually* happens it's a lot harder than we can ever expect it to be, and many good people end up quitting. Failure can feel incredibly raw and vulnerable and we naturally try to avoid that at all costs.

When you are skiing and you fall, wet snow can get in your gloves and down your back. It gets in your goggles and fogs them up. It takes time, patience, and occasionally a spare pair of gloves to swap out to continue on through the day and enjoy yourself.

How can you best endure the dips and falls of creating your Fresh Tracks? Start by developing a sense of trust in yourself— you know your next step. When you do this your intuition gets stronger and you are more able to bounce back quickly from the setbacks you are destined to experience.

Trust yourself that you'll keep trying. There is an old saying that "businesses don't go under, the owners quit." I share this statement with you and ask you to apply that to your goals. Trusting yourself that you won't quit is a key factor in success and is what differentiates those who do accomplish what they want in life from those who don't.

It's easy to lose trust in yourself and not recognize that lack of self-trust is what is going on. I have a friend, Mark, who wants to stop working his J-O-B and support himself through his coaching business. He invested in a big coaching program, KNEW the business he wanted to start and the coaching he wanted to provide was in alignment with his purpose, and excitedly quit his job and declared himself a business owner. Two months later he panicked. He had no clients, no income and the bills were piling up. He had to make a tough decision to get another job, which paid even less than the one he had before, and continue working on his new business on the side. Nine months later he found himself incredibly frustrated. He had put in place the website, basic marketing funnel and had done some online trainings (and had people attend!), but he still wasn't bringing in nearly enough money to support himself.

Mark found himself getting tired and, while having great intentions to network and meet prospects in the community, wasn't following through on his commitments and was starting to doubt his ability to make this dream a reality.

What happened? He stopped trusting himself. After that initial jump into entrepreneurship and his perceived immediate failure, he was afraid to trust himself. He didn't trust that he would make

money in his business. It came through in his daily actions...
he was partially committing, not following through, completely
sabotaging himself because he was afraid to fail again.

How long can you last?

Endurance is an essential quality for anyone who sets their
mind to cut Fresh Tracks—whether starting a new business,
achieving new and aggressive goals, or striving to accomplish
great and powerful tasks.

Endurance is the power to withstand something challenging.
The ability to do something difficult for a long time. When you
have endurance you know you can manage the consequences of
courageous personal decisions and you are willing to stick it out.

One of the main reasons people fail in cutting Fresh Tracks is
because they don't have the endurance to keep pushing through
after they fail. And most of us fail and fail and fail again! So you
can see how lack of endurance can quickly become a detrimental
factor to achieving your Fresh Tracks.

Discipline versus Endurance

Discipline and endurance are actually two separate things. You
can be incredibly disciplined and yet not be able to tolerate the
pain of endurance. Dedication, self-discipline and perseverance
are all characteristics of someone who has the ability to endure.
Here's an example of a small business owner having endurance
versus discipline.

Bailey is disciplined enough to write an article for her e-zine every week. She writes that article every week no matter what. She is disciplined enough to do this and her writing strengthens over time. After a year of doing this she did not see her subscriber base grow or her sales increase, so she decided to stop and start another project. Someone with endurance recognizes the goal of producing the e-zine is not being accomplished, so looks for other ways to achieve their goal. Examining other list-building options, trying different layouts or exploring other ways to improve engagement represents endurance. Having the determination and stick-to-itiveness to make the e-zine successful is endurance. The discipline is writing it each week.

In spite of roadblocks, successful entrepreneurs are able to keep the end goal in mind and push through their difficulties. Through time and experience, they discover and set a good pace for themselves and continue on.

Malcolm Gladwell, author of *The Outlier*, shares that it takes 10,000 hours to achieve mastery. Most people stop well before their 10,000 hours because they get bored, they don't see improvement, or they think they've "done enough" and move on to their next adventure.

HOW CAN YOU BECOME ONE OF THE FEW WHO HAS THE ENDURANCE TO STICK IT OUT UNTIL YOU ACHIEVE SUCCESS?

Endurance develops every time you reject the temptation to give up. From battling the difficulties of staying focused, to enduring unexpected expenses, handling flaky clients and maneuvering a constantly changing business economy, it's easy to reach a point where you don't think you can or should continue on.

Understand it's not when you are at the top of your game that you discover your best self. It's when you are making your way through your darkest hours that your true strength emerges. It's when most would quit and stop searching for their next step that failure sets in.

How do you build endurance? To start with, decide your ultimate end goal. Runners are known for endurance training. Their goals can often range from running faster to running farther. By determining a goal, you set yourself up to push yourself to a new place—and, as with most things new, there are growing pains! Push through the growing pains until you hit your stride. Prepare now for your goal to come true, because by the time you need to act—when the need for endurance presents itself—the time to prepare is over. The need for endurance kicks in when you are ready to quit. Start developing qualities now that will help you succeed when times are difficult.

According to Caroline Myss, author of *Entering the Castle*, "Without the capacity to endure, you are impatient, demanding, short-tempered, and you tend to abandon projects that you are meant to complete because you cannot immediately see their significance… With endurance, you know that you can survive anything that is asked of you… Endurance enables you spiritually to listen better to God, to follow your inner compass."

One key ingredient to having endurance is taking responsibility and ownership for all your results.

Taking 100 percent responsibility for your results

Until you begin to take full responsibility for your own experience of life, you have no possibility of changing it. What you take responsibility for, you can change.

It takes courage, perseverance and discipline to look at yourself, your actions, your beliefs, and take responsibility for EVERYTHING going on. This is taking ownership of where you are heading.

What does it mean to take 100 percent responsibility of everything in your life?

Whenever anything happens in your life, you don't ever blame any other person, institution or influence. That means no blaming your parents, your kids, your partner, the economy, the IRS, the bank… nothing.

This is a foundational concept that can quickly become very deep and beyond the scope of this book. I know the thought of taking TOTAL responsibility for everything that happens to you, especially the unpleasant things, can seem overwhelming. Your car gets rear-ended; how is that your responsibility? You are mugged. Your store is robbed. The list can go on and the events more violent. As you review events or events happen, look for the lesson there was/is for you to learn. Why might this have happened and what can you take away from it?

Another aspect of taking 100 percent responsibility for everything in your life is learning to forgive others. It's always easier to take responsibility for something when there is nothing to forgive. Also understand that responsibility is not blame. Not blaming others and not blaming yourself. I'm not saying this is easy, but if you can get to the place where you see the lesson in everything that happens to you, you are being empowered versus being a victim. You are in a place where you can control the only common denominator in every aspect of your life: You.

The next step in taking 100 percent responsibility for everything in your life is becoming conscious of how you approach the actions you take. What are you expecting as you begin doing something? What do you want to happen or think will happen? Simply start being aware. You don't want to expect to fail, you want to expect to win. Yet you want to expect to win with the understanding that you won't be crushed forever if you have a setback. Failing is trying, and without trying there is no succeeding.

The healthiest way to approach anything is to expect to succeed and if you don't, accept it. Let's take a look at healthy ways to accept failure.

How to accept failure

1. Don't personalize it. YOU are not your results. The stronger your spiritual self-esteem, the more you'll realize you are not how much money you have in the bank. You are not how big your debts are or how great your failures. You are not all the trophies you won in high school. You are not the car you drive. You are not the clothes you wear. You are not your failures. Conversely, you are not your successes either.

You are not what other people think of you. Results are results—don't judge them.

2. Give the perceived failed event some space. Get away from it all and surround yourself with people and places that you love. The most calming thing for me is taking a few days up in the mountains and getting out of town. One day will often do it. The fresh mountain air and the change of scenery allows me to put my life back in perspective. I can make decisions with my priorities and my big goals front and center. Go away for the weekend, spend time with family and friends, retreat from the situation and clear your head.

3. Look for the lesson or the "aha" moment from the event. Each failure makes you stronger and brings you closer to success. Each failure also has a lesson that you can take from it on how *not* to accomplish your goal. Sometimes I'll need some time and distance from the event to see what the lesson was, but it's always there. In fact, looking back over my life I can see where I had to experience failure several times before I got the lesson.

4. Be coachable and open to feedback. Find respected mentors and coaches you are comfortable being vulnerable and sharing with. Hiring coaches has been the single best thing I have done to create massive change in my life. In fact, my second coach, whom I greatly admire, told me in the beginning of our relationship I was not open and was actually not being coachable and he wouldn't coach with me unless I changed. Believe me, I changed in a heartbeat and always remember what he said! Truthfully I was complete-

ly shocked and caught off-guard; I never expected feedback like that. I am so grateful he was direct and honest with me and I went home a changed person. I still keep in mind how I was being un-coachable. I had a reason why every suggestion he offered wouldn't work and I had the perfect excuse for why my life was the way it was. When I came home from my coaching with him I started being aware of when I deflected and wasn't open. It was eye-opening to recognize that every person in my family, even my children, did the exact same thing! You can bet my kids had a very quick about-face when I recognized this way of responding to feedback! I never would have known I was so closed-minded about receiving feedback if I hadn't paid someone to give me the honest feedback I needed to change. Most people close to us either don't want to hurt our feelings and don't say anything, or aren't skilled enough to recognize what's going on.

5. Set a move-on date. Give yourself permission to wallow in misery, cry, scream, pout, hide, and eat chocolate. It's actually important you feel and release your emotion and not stuff it down and hide it. However, you can't wallow in misery forever. Feel it fully, express it in whatever manner suits you, and then move on. Depending on what happened, you may grant yourself an hour, 24 hours, maybe the weekend. It is an event that did not come out the way you wanted. Release this event and move on. Once I realize emotion is overtaking me, I quickly assess why, which also allows me to detach a bit and say out loud how long I have permission

to sulk. I'll even share it with my family. And then I go full out and let it run its course. My emotions have permission to play full out. And when it's over it's over.

6. You are not alone. First, recognize you are not the first person on the planet to start a business and have a hiccup. You are not the first person to start on a health regimen and not follow through. You are not the first person to be too afraid to ask for a divorce. Put your feelings into perspective and then find some support, even professional support if necessary. If you feel alone, surround yourself with other entrepreneurs or others striving to achieve a similar goal and find a community or a coaching group where it is comfortable to share and learn from each other. There is strength in community.

7. Pull yourself out of it. Once your time commitment has passed, you may have to do some work to get back on the happy track. You'll have to discover what works for you, and you may plan some time that first morning to really dig in and uplift your spirits. Try listening to podcasts, reading motivational books, listening to uplifting music, dancing, cooking. Go for a run or a hike in nature. Part of your self-discovery might be learning how to lift yourself up and pull yourself out of the dumps when you get down.

Failure is a judgement. One way to look at the "failing event" is to take the emotion and judgement off of it. You have to be strong to do this because the people around you probably won't have the consciousness to do it. Know that you have simply found one way (or one more way) to not accomplish what you set out to do. Similar to a science experiment with a hypothesis, procedure, and conclusion. There is no right or wrong, just an outcome.

Your results are not personal. Your results are not good or bad. They are simply results.

In-depth training from Kelly on Chapter 6 is available here: http://kellyrobbins.net/tynsadvancedmaterial/

The advanced material will give you access to a training video from Kelly, a recap of the chapter, a top tip from the chapter and a challenge for you!

Work along with the book in the *Trust Your Next Step Workbook* http://kellyrobbins.net/trust-next-step-workbook/

CHAPTER 7

BELIEVING IN YOURSELF

WHO YOU ARE SPEAKS SO LOUDLY
I CAN'T HEAR WHAT YOU ARE SAYING.

RALPH WALDO EMERSON

In order to successfully create Fresh Tracks you must believe in yourself enough to know you can do it. You have to believe your dreams are possible. Close your eyes for a moment, take a deep breath or two, and feel into your Fresh Tracks vision. Do you feel a sense of excitement and urgency to jump in and start taking action steps or do you feel a knot in your stomach and have doubt and fear running through your body?

If this thought immediately brings knots to your stomach, it's ok. It's a great awareness, and you can proactively change your views on your ability to create what you want in your life. Ask yourself honestly, "Can I do this?" If not, take a step back and start by seeing if you can believe it's possible for someone else. It does not have to be someone you know. It's tapping into that feeeeeling, that knowing, that what you wish is possible. That whatever it is you wish to accomplish CAN be done.

JK Rowling was a single mother of three on welfare when she wrote Harry Potter. From Steve Jobs and Bill Gates to Oprah Winfrey and Ursula Burns (CEO of Xerox), if you look you can find inspiration. No matter how large the odds may seem against you, accomplishing your Fresh Tracks is possible.

See if that settles you, then move on to folks around you. Is there anyone you know, even a friend of a friend who has accomplished some part of your goal? Are you able to tap in to a feeling of believing that's closer to home? The ultimate goal is to acquire a belief that achieving your goals is more than just a possibility.

Now this exploration of belief turns to you. What has to happen for you to believe in yourself? How can you quiet all those negative voices in your head? It's time to build a high sense of self-esteem because you won't be able to cut your Fresh Tracks without it.

No one is going to believe in you as much you believe in yourself. No one.

There may be times when it feels as if the entire world thinks you're crazy—and some well-intentioned people will let you know it too! You must maintain your strength and the inner knowing that you are on the right path.

How do you go about building strong self-esteem? This was the question I had to discover for myself at one point too.

KELLY'S JOURNEY INTO BUILDING SELF-ESTEEM

I am really good at getting things done. In the beginning of starting my business I was so committed to making it work I would have done anything—and I did. I followed all the formulas for creating a website, building a platform for making online sales, creating information products and services. I published an e-zine every week (for a few years I did two!), I had a podcast, I went to networking events, and I made cold calls. I was dedicated.

I would have done 300 sit-ups twice a day, run 10 miles and worn lipstick on my knees if that was what it took. As a business owner and marketer, I found myself very busy and still struggling. My personal life began to fall apart and I found myself depressed, frustrated, and not clear on what next steps I should take.

One common thing I had heard from successful people was how important it is to invest in yourself. So I did. I hired a business coach and spent an unheard of amount of money that I didn't have. I had been watching this coach for several years and trusted him. This coach had worked with many people who had become millionaires and seemed to have it all. I knew I had implemented just about every marketing tool available—and was doing them as well as I knew how to—and that there just had to be a few tweaks for me to make and I would be making millions. For all the money I was paying, I knew my coach would share with me the magic sprinkle dust you couldn't buy in a book or how-to kit. I sat in excitement for my first private coaching call with him, knowing my dreams would all come true and my bank account would be overflowing—like he did with those other millionaire clients of his. I was a hard worker and I would do it!

On our first coaching call I sat excitedly, pen in hand, ready to hear the magic formula. And you know what he told me?

It's not what you are doing, but how you are being that is causing your struggle.

I felt a wave of fear go through my entire body as I sat there. I did not know what to say. I just spent every penny I had, and every penny I was going to make all year, and the answer was not to do 20 more push-ups. WTF?

I didn't say a word for two full minutes. And neither did he. In my stunned silence, I put my pen down and looked out the window, wondering what I was going to do now. I finally asked what he meant by how I was "being." I had never heard of that before, and it didn't sound like jumping jacks or blogging.

He explained that how I was being, meaning my confidence, my self-esteem, my beliefs, all play a major role in my ability to create anything. My low confidence came across energetically in everything I did. I could say all the right words and do all the right things, yet people would feel like they didn't trust me or that something was off and they would not buy. They might not know why, but their intuition was telling them "No".

This was news to me! I have a master's degree, awards, and all the right marketing tools… why was this just now coming up? And the more important questions I had to ask were:

"How do I strengthen my confidence? Improve my self-esteem?"

That was my journey for the next year and continues to be my journey to this day. I am going to share with you a little bit of what I discovered.

NINE KEY INGREDIENTS TO BUILDING POWERFUL SELF-ESTEEM

1. Internal locus of control versus external locus of control
2. Not hiding from the truth, even if it hurts or is uncomfortable
3. Cultivating a strong spiritual self-esteem
4. Taking 100 percent responsibility for everything in life
5. Integrity with self
6. Choosing consciousness rather than unconsciousness
7. Accepting who I am: the good, bad, and the ugly
8. Asserting myself; self-advocacy
9. Living on purpose rather than drifting through life

INTERNAL LOCUS OF CONTROL VERSUS EXTERNAL LOCUS OF CONTROL

I originally learned this concept in my first college communications class when I was eighteen. I was completely fascinated with the subject. The locus of control describes your personality tendency and how your attitude and behavior affect the results in your life.

Locus means center or source. An internal locus of control is a psychological term introduced in the 1950's by Julian Rotter. A person with an internal locus of control believes they can influence events and their outcomes, while someone with an external locus of control blames outside forces for everything. Someone with an external locus of control believes luck or fate plays a role in what they achieve. Conversely, someone with a strong internal locus of control believes the effort they put into something is what yields results.

People with a strong internal locus of control tend to persevere longer and work harder in order to achieve what they want. Your locus of control says a lot about how you view the world and your beliefs on how much control you have of the outcomes. You can see how important this is if you are going out on a ledge and creating Fresh Tracks in your life!

At eighteen I had never heard of anything like this before and was fascinated with the concept. I vividly remember taking a self-assessment in class and hoping I had an internal locus of control—which I did. I have done nothing but work to build and strengthen that to this day.

I can't stress enough how important it is to at least understand what your locus of control is in living a purposeful life and taking control of your destiny. If you have a belief that things happen TO you when things get tough you'll reach a point where you say, "Why bother?" Because everything is against you and nothing you do will change things anyway.

However, if you have the belief that you control your destiny, that puts the power in your hands. We just spent an entire chapter looking at failure. How you view your failures are important. A person with an internal locus of control will fail just as much as anyone else. The difference is in how they pick themselves up, own their results (rather than blaming others) and continue on.

Now is a good time to start paying attention to automatic responses you have to events that happen. From politics and world events to bad hair days and burned dinners, whose fault is it and what can you do to change things in the future? Pay attention to your self-talk and notice when you say things like "I have no choice" or "There's nothing I can do." You always have a choice. Even not making a choice is a choice to allow other people or events to decide for you.

Not hiding from the truth, even if it hurts or is uncomfortable

We often hide the truth from ourselves because we don't want to feel the depth of the pain it causes. Calling the truth forward and facing it head on is difficult. Despite its difficulty, discovering the truth about ourselves, especially the parts we don't like and keep hidden, is imperative to walking through life consciously. Most of us don't surround ourselves with people who see the truth or have the skill to show it to us lovingly, so we can examine it and make changes if necessary.

Why don't we see the truth about ourselves? There are sides to us we do not want to show the world, often called our "shadow" or "dark" side.

We wear many masks to protect ourselves from others because we think we won't fit in, we won't be liked, or we are deep down a terrible person. We keep ourselves safe by not letting others see us, and over time we start to believe that's who we really are.

I call being aware of these tendencies in ourselves moving towards consciousness. What does it mean to be a conscious person? This word is thrown around frequently and most don't take the time to think about what it really means. Being conscious means being aware of yourself, your responses, your emotional reactions, your fears, and how you react to certain people and situations.

And taking consciousness a step further, which actions and responses are not the characteristics of the new you? The you who has stepped in to the Fresh Tracks you are creating? For example, the Kelly who first quit her corporate job and started a freelance copywriting business and made practically nothing is a completely different person than the one who brought in $50,000 a year part-time. I had to change who I was to change my results. And that Kelly is different from the Kelly who writes best-selling books and travels around the country leading workshops and speaking.

To not hide from the truth, you have to be able to take an honest look at behaviors and beliefs that do not support the new you. This may not feel good. I shared the example earlier of the coach who showed me I was deflecting his comments, not receiving his advice. I cried when he told me that. When he told me I was almost un-coachable, I realized how serious the situation was. I did not want that or I would be stuck where I was forever— and I was miserable! I chose him as my coach because I trusted him and that is why I knew I could believe what he said about me. I was at rock bottom when I started the coaching program with him and was incredibly clear about one thing… I did not know what I was doing that was not yielding me the results I desired and I did not know what to do next.

When the time came for me to trust my next step it was to hire him and his team.

The day he shared with me that I was being un-coachable I was in a room with about 14 other entrepreneurs. I was shaking in fear the entire time I was in the room, knowing my turn was coming for him to focus on me. After some training in the morning he went around the room and did what we call laser coaching with each person, and I was last. He asked each person questions and coached them and gave feedback. Being in the room I was able to witness what he was seeing and agree with everything he said to them. I knew he was right and I was learning new things at the same time.

When it did finally get to be my turn and he shared what he shared with me, I knew it was true, even though I didn't want to believe it and didn't want to hear it. I had watched him be right with the other 14 people in the room and had no choice but to believe him. He wouldn't be right with everyone but me!

It was with love that he gave each person what they needed to hear so they could be in alignment with Universal Law. It was in love that he shared the truths that most of us couldn't see on our own. Truths we needed to acknowledge and heal before we could see the world through a healthy and changed lens. What a gift to share with people in such a way! A way I also strive to share with my clients.

Your job right now is to be open to seeing the truth about yourself. What truths are you hiding from to keep yourself safe? Are you open to finding someone you can trust to give you the feedback you need to hear, and be open to receiving it? This person should not be a family member or a close friend. It needs be someone skilled enough to lead you to examine your subconscious beliefs, without being manipulated by your ego, to see the truth and be honest and direct enough to tell you. That's what a mentor does.

You have to want this so much you hunt it down, pay for it, and do whatever it takes to become aware of the truth. The truth of how you are being right now is what has gotten you to this place in your life.

Cultivating Spiritual Self-Esteem

Self-esteem means having confidence in your worth and abilities. Having self-respect. Synonyms for esteem are reverence, admire, appreciate, worship, idolize, respect… how often does your self-talk include thoughts like these?

This chapter is about examining our beliefs about life, about events, about possibilities, including those beliefs about ourselves. If you're anything like I was, my self-talk consisted of me beating myself up, not being very forgiving, in fact being down right mean, and judgmental. I said things to myself I would never in a million years say to my worst enemy.

The awareness of my self-talk shined a light on how I really thought about myself. Not very highly!

So what does it mean to have spiritual self-esteem? I first heard this term when I heard Dr. Roger Teel talk. I loved it! I immediately glommed onto it and explored what this term means to me and why it is so important.

Spiritual self-esteem is a way of experiencing the self as more than the body you occupy. I like to look at it as I am a SOUL with a body, not that I am human being with a soul. I find this knowing incredibly empowering! Being able to tap into a mighty something that is much bigger, wiser and all-knowing than me has been a complete game-changer in my life.

Spiritual self-esteem has helped me have confidence in myself and my abilities by changing my belief that I am just a mom with three kids with an endless road of mistakes and mountains that can't be conquered. It meant changing my belief that all those other people succeeding in life are different than me. Those successful people and I are made of the same substance and come from the same place. I don't consider myself a religious person at all. In fact, a mere five years ago the word God only came out of my mouth when I stubbed my toe. And it was usually followed by a "dammit." I had reached an incredibly low point in my life and was working diligently to dig myself out when I started to explore spirituality and the role I played in a larger Universe. At my rock bottom I was completely broke, my ex-husband had moved out for about two years, nothing in my life had changed (which I was sure it would!), and my teenage kids were struggling. I was bone tired and depressed and willing to do anything to change my circumstances. I knew I did not put myself and the kids through a divorce and a move for things to stay crappy and was determined to figure out what was going on.

Taking an honest look at the role I had played in getting myself stuck where I was, delving into a twelve-step program, and an honest hard-working year with a good therapist were huge. Hiring a business coach, taking a few personal development programs, and studying the fact that there just might be something else to me than this body were all a huge crossroad in my journey.

The spiritual piece was key to improving my self-esteem because I could get there is a force, an energy that is behind all things and that we are all connected. It made my failures not as much about me personally, but more about the actions I was taking. How I was doing things. I can change how I do things—what I think, how I respond—especially if there is a force, a power I can tap into that is bigger than me. It's not about saying I haven't made mistakes, because I clearly did and still do! But developing an understanding that I have access to an unlimited supply of a powerful, positive, loving force, was huge. It simply felt good and I felt lighter. Understanding that who I am is not defined by my past is incredibly empowering. Embodying the fact that we are all interconnected helped me develop an unshakable confidence that I am absolutely supposed to be here. I found that conviction freeing and empowering. My studies continue to this day.

Days may come when you cannot see how you are going to create your Fresh Tracks. You may wonder how you will even take that next step on your path when it feels so long and laborious. It might feel like the world is against you and you bit off more than you can chew. On those days—and they will come—try to feel into what faith means to you. The work you do, the love and joy you have to share, is God, Source, The Universe, energy working through you. It's not you, it's that force. It needs you to express itself. Everyone needs you to express yourself, in fact there are people waiting for you to step up so they can follow.

There is a power in knowing and embracing this truth that I have not been able to get anywhere else.

Taking 100 percent responsibility for everything

The very crux of this statement is that you have the power to change anything. Anything. You may not like the options you have, but you have them. And knowing you can change any situation, any action, any direction is empowering! Being empowered is a liberating, freeing feeling. In order to embrace the weight of being empowered there may be some things you need to let go of first.

For some of us, this means letting go of victim stories we have. A terrific book that does an excellent job breaking apart this concept is *Radical Forgiveness* by Colin Tipping. Forgiving others plays a huge role in many aspects of our lives and is a book and point of study in and of itself. In Tipping's book he examines the effects not forgiving has on us from a physical and an emotional standpoint. He also takes a stand that the major experiences and relationships we have, and often repeat, are there because we have chosen the experience in order to learn a lesson or heal a wound. On a soul level we continue to bring people into our lives and repeat patterns until we heal the wound. Examples of wounds are: Struggling to commit in relationships. Struggling to speak your truth, staying silent when you have something to say. Continuously giving your power away to others.

In the book there are exercises and examples of how we create stories out of situations, usually stemming from an instance when we are young. The people we are angry at or who are seemingly creating awful and painful situations for us are really there as our teachers to help us heal a wound. Even to the extremes of abusive relationships, neglectful parents, bullies, or even rape. This is taking 100 percent responsibility for everything that happens in your life to an extreme. What a powerful and loving place to stand in. No victim mentality or stories here at all!

Know you always have the power to get it right, to make it different, to change things up. You haven't been using that power for whatever reason…you want to feel safe, you need to be right, you didn't know…now you do and you have a choice to look at creating your outcomes differently now.

How do you know if you are taking 100 percent responsibility for your results or not?

▶ There are reasons (otherwise called excuses) for why you do things or do not do things

▶ It's someone else's fault

▶ It's hard to follow through on activities

▶ You deserve better and you are not working for it, and you think other people should do it for you

▶ You know your life will be better when you have _____

▶ You feel strongly that someone else should fix your life

When you have strong self-esteem and take 100 percent responsibility for everything in your life, if things don't turn out the way you desire you will be empowered enough to ask, "How did I do that? What can I do differently? What did I do or not do? What did I say or not say to have the other person respond that way? What were my beliefs that got me to this place and what do I need to change?"

Do you see the difference?

INTEGRITY WITH SELF

Do you pride yourself on being a person of your word? Are you 100 percent confident when you make a commitment to someone that you'll keep it? Do you see yourself as dependable so that people can count on you? Do you take pride in that? Keeping your word is an admirable trait and something to be earned and respected.

Even people who are usually dependable slip just a little on things that don't seem as important. Such as promising to follow-up and not doing it. Or giving a fake name or phone number to receive an e-zine or free information. Oftentimes we make small social commitments to please people and don't place much value on them once we leave the situation. For example, "I'll call you sometime" or "Let's meet for coffee soon." These are examples of being in integrity with others and is what most often comes to mind when we speak of integrity.

An important distinction here is how you treat yourself.

How often do you keep your word to yourself? How many times have you sworn off alcohol or chocolate and found yourself baking a cake with Bailey's Irish Cream two days later? Can you name the number of times you have set New Year's resolutions and not kept them? Made a commitment to work out three days a week? Quit eating chocolate? Never, ever, ever get back together with THAT guy? Promise to keep your cool around your drunk uncle?

It seems harmless to not keep your word to yourself because no one knows but you. You aren't harming anyone; no one else is involved.

The promises you make to yourself are actually the most important. We keep our word to other people more than we do to ourselves because it matters to us more what other people think of us than it does what we think of ourselves.

Keeping and honoring your word to yourself is an important step in strengthening your belief in yourself, in raising your self-esteem, and creating Fresh Tracks. The truth is, you may keep your word with other people, honor your commitments, and be a completely honest person...until it comes to yourself.

YOUR WORD IS LAW

That is a powerful and accurate statement. Your word is law. What you say, IS. Particularly what you say out loud. So be especially careful what you say. What comes out of your lips is vitally important, as it sets Universal Law in motion. You create more of what you say.

Being impeccable with your word is a lifelong skill, so give yourself some time and grace as you incorporate being vigilant with your word into your daily life. You are literally changing a lifetime of beingness and it starts with your commitment, your willingness to be aware, and coming from a place of love for yourself and the journey you are on.

The truth is that when we make promises or commitments to ourselves and don't keep them, we learn to NOT trust ourselves. Ultimately, we stop believing in ourselves and what we say. We cannot manifest our desires from ease while in this space. We say things and make commitments to ourselves and don't think twice about it because we've done it so many times.

It's important to build the muscle of integrity and begin the process of strengthening our word to ourselves. One exercise is to make a commitment to yourself, something small, and keep it. Make the commitment over fourteen days and make it uncomfortable and out of the ordinary but not huge. An example may be going outside every day at exactly noon and doing five jumping jacks. Or moving ten rocks across your yard and then putting them back, one at a time, at four am.

The important takeaway here is be very, very cautious about what promises you make. Especially those you make to yourself. Rule of thumb—make very few promises and treat them with reverence. No matter what, keep your word.

ACCEPTING WHO I AM, THE GOOD, BAD AND THE UGLY

Self-acceptance is a positive outlook on who you really are inside. That has nothing to do with accolades, awards or accomplishments. When you accept yourself, you are able to not only recognize but also embrace your weaknesses as well as your strengths. Self-acceptance is different than self-esteem in that self-esteem refers to how valuable you think you are. Self-acceptance is accepting yourself just as you are without thinking you need to change anything about yourself. It's getting to know who you are beyond the clothes you wear, the job you hold, your story, or how other people see you.

Part of learning to accept yourself is to become aware of the self-judgements you've adopted to cope with life. One example of a self-judgement is if you identify with being a perfectionist. Perfectionists have learned to set high standards for themselves and focus on being good and getting things right. There is a lot of judgement in that. You are judging what is good versus what is bad. You are also judging what is right and wrong. One way to look at the effects of your life is to not judge them as good or bad, but simply see the results. Judgement is based on perspective—yours. My judgement of good or bad will be quite different.

If you can identify instances where you are judging yourself and learn to be kind and accepting instead, you can learn to build awareness of the real you inside and the ultimate goodness and love that you are.

Rejecting yourself is a common way many of us go through life. When we reject ourselves, we tend to put ourselves last and not make time for ourselves.

When you reject yourself, you go through life sure that everyone else will reject you too, so you people please, try not to be a burden, don't ask for anything, ultimately you feel unlovable no matter how much you try to love someone else. The self-rejection causes you to be mean to yourself. We say terrible things to ourselves, we judge, we compare ourselves to others, we are incredibly self-critical and don't forgive mistakes. We wallow in shame. We would never allow our friends to be treated this way, yet many of us spend each day rejecting every thought, every action, every interaction with judgement and rejection.

When your self-acceptance is low, when you are anxious and doubt yourself, you become indecisive and play it safe. You don't trust yourself because you are not connected to the real you. To accept means to receive. As we talk about self-acceptance, we are talking about you accepting the real you.

What has to happen for you to embrace and even love the real you? Start with creating a gratitude practice—be grateful for at least one thing every day. Choose a different thing about yourself each day to focus on. It can be as simple as "I am grateful for my feet that walk me around my house" or "I am grateful for my eyes, that I am able to read this book."

Another big choice that leads to self-acceptance is taking time to recognize and focus on what you HAVE done. Begin to notice all the things you accomplish each day, or over the course of a year. Change how you look at yourself consciously. A best practice for both the gratitude exercise and focusing on what you have done is to write it down or mentally review accomplishments each night before you go to bed. Do it while you brush your teeth or take a shower. Make conscious choices about how you focus on yourself.

ASSERTING MYSELF—SELF-ADVOCACY

Assertiveness is knowing who you are, what you stand for, and then having the ability to express that in everyday interactions with people. Being assertive is not about being aggressive. Aggressive people force their opinion on others and leave others feeling attacked, whereas assertive people state their opinions in a respectful manner. Aggressive people make others feel ignored or attacked.

When you aren't assertive, you may be passive and you may feel like your needs are not being met and become hurtful and angry.

What does it look like when you are assertive? You let other people know what you want without making vague requests. You speak up when you have an opinion. And you are not afraid to stand up for yourself. People often don't assert themselves because they want to avoid conflict. That can look like agreeing too quickly, or passively making their way through life. Watch out though, these people can easily become bitter or passive-aggressive because their needs are not being met. Assertiveness can be as simple as stating which restaurant you'd like to go to for dinner or returning clothes you purchased two weeks ago that are already falling apart. Or saying no to a family member who consistently borrows money and never pays you back.

Asserting yourself is an important aspect to believing in yourself and your ability to cut Fresh Tracks. It is essential for self-care, high self-esteem and self-integrity. It is your ability to take care of yourself in the world.

Self-advocacy is about you taking empowering steps to be in charge of your life and your results. Examples may be being proactive about getting the information you need to make an informed decision, knowing your rights and responsibilities, and asking for help when you need it.

LIVING ON PURPOSE RATHER THAN DRIFTING THROUGH LIFE

People who live their lives on purpose find activities that mean something to them and spend most of their time in those activities.

Finding meaning in life rather than going through the motions of each day can be what gives you direction and a sense of meaning to your life. It is the opposite of living the numb life. Living a life of purpose gives you a reason why. Why you get up each day. Why you love life.

Knowing your why gives you a reason to go on. Other folks may be working towards the same goal, but lack the passion and endurance to achieve it because they don't have a strong reason why. They are just doing it to do it and that can get boring quickly! Knowing your why can add passion and determination to each day. Imagine waking up each morning knowing you are on the right path, regardless of what anyone else says. It brings enthusiasm and excitement to each day and can also be what motivates you to confront difficulties and overcome obstacles that may have otherwise stopped you. When you are living with purpose you are more likely to be passionate about what you do. And there's something about passion that lights a fire within each of us. It makes us happy. We are more likely to smile, and studies have shown that people actually age better when they live with purpose.

There is a time and place for healing old wounds, evaluating past wrongs, and recognizing unhealthy blocks and patterns in our lives. It's imperative you understand that the elimination of hurts and negative thoughts does not by default yield a positive result. Just like the lack of depression does not guarantee happiness, nor does the absence of abuse guarantee love. Building positive self-confidence and a healthy self-esteem requires you to be a self-motivated self-starter, and to go make it happen for you. Confidence, happiness, self-love, integrity and assertiveness all require you to generate the energy to go create it for yourself. It is the next step on the road to creating your Fresh Tracks.

In-depth training from Kelly on Chapter 7 is available here:
http://kellyrobbins.net/tynsadvancedmaterial/

The advanced material will give you access to a training video from Kelly, a recap of the chapter, a top tip from the chapter and a challenge for you!

Work along with the book in the *Trust Your Next Step Workbook*
http://kellyrobbins.net/trust-next-step-workbook/

CHAPTER 8

WHO ARE YOU SKIING WITH? THE ROLE RELATIONSHIPS PLAY IN FRESH TRACKS

LOTS OF PEOPLE WANT TO RIDE WITH YOU IN THE LIMO, BUT
WHAT YOU WANT IS SOMEONE WHO WILL TAKE THE BUS WITH YOU
WHEN THE LIMO BREAKS DOWN.

OPRAH WINFREY

In addition to the goals you set and the choices you make, who you surround yourself with plays an important factor in your ability to cut Fresh Tracks.

ARE YOUR RELATIONSHIPS UNCONSCIOUSLY AFFECTING YOUR LIFE?

Have you spent thousands of hours working on yourself and striving for more in life? Have you ever had a vision and just gone all out for it? We invest in our personal growth and development. We hire coaches, seek out mentors. We may even do yoga or change our diet, begin exercising to put ourselves in a different, happier, more productive space. We read books and attend trainings to discover what our next steps are to achieving happiness and success.

We strive to hone our skills and strengthen our energy, and yet it doesn't stick. We continue to struggle to achieve our goals, which seem to be right in front of us at times and then we lose it! The goals we KNOW are in alignment with our purpose and passion and that are rightfully ours are seemingly always a step or two away.

One often overlooked area that is right in front of us every day and in fact often negates all the work we do, is the people we surround ourselves with.

Who you surround yourself with is one of the most important factors to your keeping and achieving success. We are going to spend some time determining if a relationship is healthy or toxic, examining the different types of relationships you want to create, and deciding when to keep and when to lovingly let go of some relationships.

IDENTIFYING TOXIC RELATIONSHIPS

How do you know if a relationship is healthy or toxic? If you are being physically abused or there is blatant infidelity, the toxicity is obvious. However, toxic relationships are often less easy to spot when those factors are not involved, yet the toxicity is just as valid. Often we are in toxic relationships and aren't even aware of it.

Toxic relationships affect your health, your self-esteem, and they counter every step you take forward in your personal development journey. Not only that, they can lead to stress, depression, even physical health issues.

Toxic relationships can come in many forms and are not always recognizable as toxic: parents, siblings, coworkers, spouses, children, friends, coaches, partners, and bosses can all be harmful.

If you can answer yes to more than five of these characteristics, you are in a toxic relationship:

▶ You are always walking on eggshells.

▶ You change your mood based on how the other person is being.

▶ You are afraid to speak your truth.

▶ You feel you live in constant judgement. It can be little things like what you wear, what you eat, what you say, who your friends are.

▶ You find yourself isolated from your friends and family.

▶ The other person takes more energy and rarely if ever gives any energy or attention to you.

▶ The person is narcissistic—always reflecting themselves off of you. You are a reflection of them and not your own person.

▶ You find yourself changing your opinion to please someone else.

▶ Your partner won't talk about important issues—for example, if you bring something up your partner leaves for a few days.

- ▶ There is a lack of trust.
- ▶ The person displays overt jealousy.
- ▶ You feel you don't deserve any better.
- ▶ You can't do anything right.
- ▶ You are under constant criticism.
- ▶ The relationship is filled with drama and angst.
- ▶ You feel like you have to change who you are to make them happy.
- ▶ After you spend time with them you feel worse, not better.
- ▶ When you are with the person you feel drained and tired, not energized and happy.
- ▶ The relationship is not give and take. You are always giving and they are always taking.
- ▶ When you are with them, your stomach hurts, you get a headache or another physical symptom.
- ▶ They are in control of all the money, the car or other resources.

The first step to changing a toxic relationship is to recognize you are in one. Awareness is a choice and if you are not sure, speak with a professional. We all deserve to be treated with love, respect and compassion. Period. If the people closest to us aren't treating us that way we won't treat ourselves that way. Being in a toxic relationship leads to an incredibly low self-esteem, and as much work as you do to grow as an individual, the relationship is sabotaging every step you take. Recognition is key and because the toxicity can sneak up on you, it's important to choose to be aware of it and acknowledge its presence.

Once you start to recognize the toxic behavior, you have to address it. Seeing it and not addressing it is being out of integrity with yourself. Begin to address the unacceptable behavior as it comes up.

Be clear and direct with the toxic person specifically about what they said or did and how it isn't how you wish to be treated. If the person's behavior or the situation doesn't change, you need to distance yourself from this person and set boundaries. This may mean seeing family less frequently or lovingly letting go of some long-time friends.

When you think about your relationships, what might first come to mind is your partner, children and immediate family. And there is absolutely no doubt these people play an integral role in where you are today. Books have been written on the subject and the self-healing involved in examining these relationships is something I believe all of us should examine on the roadway to conscious living. They are in our lives from a young age for a reason!

However, beyond that, in order to maintain the higher energy of the work we do—to set a goal, achieve it, and keep it so we embody that new space of being—we need to take a look at ALL of our relationships and make conscious choices about who we let into our space.

Your friends are a great example. It can be wonderful having lifelong friends, friends that you've known since childhood. There is a familiarity, a security and a comfort in spending time with them. But odds are the you who met them 20 years ago is not the same person you are today—especially if you are consciously involved in personal growth and development.

If you have any long-time friends like this, I encourage you to take time now to evaluate if these friends know you as you were or as you are now. How do you feel after you spend time with them?

WHAT DOES A HEALTHY RELATIONSHIP LOOK LIKE?

We looked at toxic relationships and what we don't want in our life. An important aspect to unhealthy relationships is recognizing what a healthy relationship looks like and gaining clarity on what you want to intentionally attract into your life. It's worthwhile to be as clear as possible on what you DO want as it is what you don't. Here are a few ideas to get you started. You feel:

► Comfortable sharing your ideas

► Secure and safe

► Able to be yourself, even when opinions differ

► Love

► Energized

► Good about yourself after you leave

► Respected

► Free to speak, share and think

► Listened to

► Trust

Other traits of healthy relationships are:

► Feelings are shared openly and honestly

► Conflicts are dealt with head-on and then dropped

- ▶ Both people understand that self-care is vital
- ▶ You want to be together
- ▶ Encourage other friendships
- ▶ Support one another
- ▶ Treat each other with respect, even when disagreeing

Protecting and controlling your energy is vital to your growth and success—and yes, that means guarding who you allow to enter your space.

As you grow, it's normal and healthy that the people you surround yourself with change, too.

It's up to you to make conscious choices on the people you permit in your space. You may need to go and find new relationships that push you to grow and stretch yourself.

TYPES OF RELATIONSHIPS

Now that we can see the difference between healthy and toxic relationships, and can agree we want to let go of or significantly reduce toxic relationships and increase healthy relationships, let's take a look at the different types of relationships most of us have in our life:

1. Family
2. Personal friends
3. Business friends/acquaintances
4. Relationship with money

FAMILY

You are stuck with your family of origin. You can't trade them for a newer model. While you may love your family, you may not enjoy how you feel when you are with them. They will always be your family and are here to stay. Recognize if you always leave them feeling drained, don't enjoy spending time with them, feel like you are always trying to get attention, or are seeking love or kudos but no one really cares. It's important to understand you can't change them but you can change YOU. It's up to you to manage what you share with them. What you expect from each encounter is in your control.

I believe our families set the groundwork for our greatest life lessons from childhood. For most of us it is well worth our time to look at what lessons we set ourselves up to experience and learn from, and then master in our lifetime. What role did our family of origin play in this? My assumption is a very large role!

Here's an example; if you were raised in a family where children were to be seen and not heard, and you learned to not be seen in order to stay out of trouble, as an adult you may still struggle with being seen. Perhaps at work you speak and people don't always listen, or you get passed up for promotions frequently. Or you might get up and speak on stage but no one remembers a single word you said (you know who you are!). As an adult, and often in your pursuit of your purpose, you will probably find that you struggle with this issue. You need to master being seen and heard to be successful in pursuing your purpose. If you grew up in an abusive home or were afraid frequently, you may have learned to become invisible to keep safe. Being invisible does not serve most adults. Especially Fresh Trackers! People pleasing, accepting one-way relationships, and not advocating for yourself are a few of the ways we fall into the trap of invisibility.

While being invisible itself does not serve us, growing out of being invisible and stepping proudly into being seen does. You can look at it as a great gift your family blessed you with. As much as you are invisible, you have in you the ability to be seen just as much.

This area is so personal and unique to each of us that in some instances it can be worthwhile to have a good therapist or a coach to help you see the gifts your family did bring to you. This does not mean you need to see a therapist for the rest of your life! Go prepared with questions you would like answered and be open to being honest and learning about yourself so you can be aware of and tackle some of these presents you gifted yourself in this life. The growth you step into IS a gift.

PERSONAL FRIENDS

Make a list of the 10 people you spend the most time with, outside of family. Who are your friends that you spend time with socially? That you call when you need to talk or just to shoot the shit? How do you feel after you spend time with them? Are they interested in the same things you are or are they your friends because they always have been?

A friendship is between two equal people, peers. Taking an inventory of the people you spend time with allows you to evaluate what type of energy you are allowing in your space. The late author Jim Rohn states "You are the sum of the five people you spend the most time with." Are these friends who you choose to be?

This is not to say your friends should be the same as you, however, they should be a positive and supportive influence on you. Are they conscious individuals interested in growth? Are they positive members of society? Most importantly, do you feel drained or energized after you spend time with them? Do you find yourself thinking about things they said or did after the fact? Maybe a subtle (or not so subtle) dig at you comes up each time you interact? Do you find yourself making excuses for things they say and do, such as "They didn't mean it?" A friend who drains you mentally, financially or emotionally is not good for you—they are NOT friends.

One characteristic of a toxic friendship is that you feel you can't get out of the situation. Perhaps you've been friends since a young age or that person has no one else to turn to and needs you. The truth is, friendships should be a 50/50 relationship and both parties should feel heard and respected, not ridiculed, belittled or used after each encounter. If your friend is always in a drama, always talking about herself, and speaks more than she listens, the friendship may be one-sided and not balanced.

Take an honest look at each of the people on your friendship list. If it feels right, some of the people you can simply spend less time with. Putting some distance between friends is OK. Relationships come and go in everyone's life and that includes friendships, not just romantic relationships.

Other friendships you may just need to sever. If you try setting boundaries with your toxic friends and they aren't honored, or you point out incidences where they are jabbing at you or cutting you down and they don't make adjustments then they need to be let go. YOU come first.

As you create your Fresh Tracks, walk through your fears and create a life filled with love, freedom and abundance, you will be changing who you are, how you feel, and ultimately how you are being. You are doing hard work to raise your consciousness and be more of who you are meant to be. No one but you can both raise and protect your energy or your mood. Who you surround yourself with has an immediate and lasting effect on who you are, and ultimately, where you go.

A great example of this is my stepson, Jack. He is a very skilled baseball player and has been on several baseball teams throughout his life. One year he joined a new team that allowed him to pitch more often and experience a different level of playing. However, his playing started being inconsistent, he was irritable at home and struggling a little bit in school. After several months, we realized how negative his teammates were—about everything! The energy of the entire team, even the parents, was a psychic drain. Drama, gossip and unsupportive behaviors were the norm. Jack made the decision to start over with a new team the next year that may not have as many wins, but has a positive, supportive energy to it.

IF I LET ALL MY FRIENDS GO, HOW DO I MAKE NEW FRIENDS?

This is a terrific question and a genuine concern. First things first. Your job is to protect your energy with your life, and that includes your personal friends. KNOW you are better off being by yourself than with someone toxic.

When I say protect your energy with your life, I mean that literally. You want to cut Fresh Tracks and create wonderful things in your life, so why let negativity or the passive aggressive behavior of other people counter your efforts? I personally work diligently to recognize negative self-talk, I am aware of what I put in my mind—from books I read to television shows I watch—why would I let another person ruin all that? I surround myself with beautiful things and wonderful smells because I am beautiful and wonderful. I eat healthy foods and exercise to take care of my physical body so I feel good. I surround myself with people who respect me and themselves. People who lift me up and who I can do the same for. If I feel something or someone bring me down, they go. And they go quickly. I don't want all my hard work demolished because of someone else's lack of consciousness.

Start by eliminating all toxic friendships, those that have run their course and you have just been hanging on to so you won't be alone. Let go of everyone who leaves you feeling bad about yourself or drained. By doing this you stop allowing in negativity. Imagine a bathtub you are filling with hot water and the drain is wide open. You can't fill the tub high enough to get in and enjoy your bath because the water is flowing out almost as fast as it is coming in. By putting a stopper on the drain you are allowing the hot water to stay in and fill up so you can get in and enjoy your bath. Just like by eliminating unhealthy friendships, you are allowing the positive, forward-moving vibration of consciousness to take root.

There may be a space between when the old friends leave and the new ones come in and you feel lonely.

Loneliness is sadness that you have no friends or company. Have you ever found yourself in the middle of a party and felt lonely? You can be in a romantic relationship or married and feel lonely. This feeling of loneliness does not have to be associated with you being alone. Let's be clear on that.

Now you have space. And you will be alone more as you let these unhealthy relationships go. Learn to be alone without being lonely and become friends with yourself before you frantically search out your new best friend.

I recommend becoming comfortable being alone. Learning to be alone can be scary at first, but soon becomes the cornerstone to your personal growth and development. Discovering how to become comfortable with yourself, how to listen to your intuition, discovering what you do and don't like, are all keys to uncovering the authentic you. Being alone with your thoughts might scare you—it does for many.

Being comfortable being alone has nothing to do with being introverted or extroverted. Being alone is a physical state. Being lonely is a feeling that some know how to deal with and others don't. We all experience it at points in our life, having the tools to recognize it and work our way out of it is important to our self-esteem and ultimately the strength we bring to our friendships.

BUSINESS FRIENDS AND ACQUAINTANCES

The next place to take a look is your business friends—you

have some, right? This is specifically a different role than your personal friends. Your business friends should be consciously hand-chosen professionals, both in and out of your industry, and ideally be in a place you want to go.

Do you find yourself chatting it up with your business friends and it's the same conversation repeatedly? Do you find you are spending your time giving advice rather than getting it? These are not your ideal business friends.

Your business friends should stretch you. What were the last three books or resources recommended to you by them? Are their businesses larger than yours and are you learning from them? Is your dream to start your own business? If so, then I recommend you start hanging around with other entrepreneurs.

When I started my freelance copywriting business, one of the first things I did was ask the Executive Director at the Business Marketing Association, an organization I had belonged to for several years at my corporate job, who was the best freelance copywriter around. She gave me a name and I called this woman and asked her out to coffee so I could pick her brain. She was busy and cancelled a few times. I kept following up with her until we finally met. I had a list of questions I had written down ahead of time and made sure our meeting was productive, short, and that I was respectful of her time. She was incredibly generous with her time, and the information she shared made a big difference in my career path as a writer. Conversely, whenever anyone, including college students, calls The Copywriting Institute just to learn about the industry or hear from me on what I did and how I make money, I freely give away the information and am happy to help. Don't be afraid to ask questions and seek out those who have achieved what you strive for. Steve Jobs talked about the importance of asking, and in fact said that one of the big reasons he got where he was is because he asked. No one that he asked told him no.

HOW TO CULTIVATE BUSINESS FRIENDSHIPS

Let's start by defining that your social media network does not make qualified business friends.

There are acquaintances and there are friends you can call with questions and for brainstorming sessions. Your professional network will have weak and strong connections. Strong connections are your co-workers, clients, and professional associates. Weak connections may be social media connections, people you met once and didn't see again, or acquaintances.

I have up-leveled my professional friends most quickly through professional coaching. I hired coaches who included group trainings and events. Not only do you share intimately in a coaching group, but you generally find yourself surrounded with business people at about the same level as you or a little higher. Some of my closest personal friends have come from coaching groups I've been in because we have several things in common.

Mastermind groups can be another way to strengthen your business connections. It's well worth it to invest in yourself and pay to join one. Surround yourself with others who know the value of self-improvement.

Networking groups can be a place to cultivate business friendships, however, buyer beware! Not all networking groups are created equal. Watch the energy of the room, the quality and variety of businesses represented, and trust your gut. Do not quickly spend money to join a group until you have gone to several meetings.

Professional Associations can be great for both the self-employed and employees. I joined the Colorado Business Marketing Association when I worked at UPS just to be around marketing minds who didn't work at UPS. My life and mind needed some fresh ideas and juju outside of my day-to-day world. Some of the relationships I made through that group have lasted decades.

Two words of caution here:

1. If you are an entrepreneur, make friends both inside and outside of your industry. For example, if you are plumber it's going to be comfortable hanging around with other plumbers. There is growth and fresh ideas in hanging around other types of businesses, so don't stick exclusively to your industry.

2. If you have a job and want to start your business, find people doing what you want to do. If you have never been around entrepreneurs before, find some to hang around with. You'll pick up information by osmosis and you'll be physically moving into the energy of what you want to create!

A special note about making money. ### It's all about being in *relationships* with people.

Last year I studied prosperity. It was my "word of the year" and I delved into it like nothing else. I took classes, I read books, I did healing work around specific words I had a charge with (opulence was one) and one of the biggest understandings I came to was that making money is directly related to being in relationship with other people.

Consider how much of your life right now is dedicated to relationships that have to do with money. Your work, employer and clients are all engaged in your relationship to money. Spending money involves being in relationship with others as well. Going to the grocery store, purchasing clothes, even going out to eat all involve other people and the giving and exchanging of money and energy. We need each other to handle our financial affairs.

Creating healthy relationships in your life affects many things. Your health. Your happiness. And now I'm including your income.

Karen Russo, author of *The Money Keys* has a wonderful exercise where she has you write down the ten people closest to you. Family, friends, etc. Then, in a column next to their name write down their estimated wealth. How many of them have the lifestyle you desire? Income? Freedom? Travel? Community? Contribution to society? What books have they read lately? What role does spirituality play?

This exercise is done to bring awareness to whom you spend your time with, whom you are in relationship with, and their relationship with money.

CREATING CHANGE GRACEFULLY

Now that you have done a deep evaluation of the different relationships in your life, you may be thinking you are ready to make a few conscious changes. There is a graceful way to do this.

Start with spending less time with those people who are

unhealthy for you. Depending on the person and your relationship, you may decide to have a conscious conversation. It depends on your relationship, how you think they'll react, and honestly, how you feel about having the conversation. Once this is done, you have made room for the new relationships you are ready to create. Nature abhors a vacuum, and I promise your friends or business acquaintance relationship groups won't stay empty forever. Here are a few steps you can take to create healthy relationships with intention:

a. Clean house. Sweep out the corners, dust the cobwebs. Take out the trash and change the burned-out lightbulbs. Get your side of the street clean.

b. Get clarity on what kind of relationships you do want. Envision how you feel, what you share, what you have to give and would like to receive from each of the relationship categories.

c. Start going to different places to meet different types of people. Consider joining a coaching group. Don't be afraid to invest in yourself—you are your most important investment! If you have goals to be around people who live a healthier lifestyle, join a hiking group or a ski club. Going by yourself and forcing yourself to make new friends can be a character-building exercise and eliminates the crutch of hiding out with your old friends.

FROM HOMELESS TO THRIVING, THIS FRESH TRACKER CHANGED HER LIFE BY TAKING CHARGE OF THE RELATIONSHIPS IN HER LIFE.

Fresh Tracker Katie got her life on track by taking charge of the relationships in her life. As an unemployed, homeless mother of an infant, Katie found herself stuck in an abusive relationship with no way out. At the lowest point in her life, Katie felt she only had the power to be upset and focus on what she didn't like about her situation. A child of two alcoholic parents, Katie grew up surrounded by unhealthy role models and abuse. Her entire life she felt unattractive and as if her life was 100 percent out of her control. It took an eviction notice for Katie to finally realize she was the only one who has the power to change herself. At the same time she had the rude awakening that she had given all her power to her husband.

Many women just like Katie go from one bad relationship to another simply because it is what they know. It's the only role modeling they've seen and, growing up in a feeling of powerlessness, it is what they naturally recreate in their lives. Katie married young, at 17, and quickly found herself in a powerless situation. When she was laid off, the man she loved and trusted wanted her to stay home and raise their son and not work. She trusted him to make the right decisions, yet slowly realized she had become stuck and unhappy. Her husband seemed to always have money for himself, yet creditors were calling every day and she was struggling to have enough money for food. She didn't feel qualified to find a job and was scared to go against her husband. An eviction notice is what gave her the strength and determination to seek change.

I asked Katie how she had the ability to turn her life around when so many people don't. Katie told me one of the most instrumental changes she made on her road to healing was learning what a healthy relationship looked like and building a support system for herself. She started by eliminating toxic relationships, including the toughest one—her husband—and setting healthy boundaries with family members who had never had boundaries before. Katie experienced an immediate increase in self-awareness after she made these adjustments, and it spurred her to keep making changes.

Katie also shared she had several lessons in the importance of networking and understanding that she didn't have to go through life alone. Both were huge game changers in her life and her son's life. Learning to ask for help from neighbors, helping out by picking up others' kids from school and seemingly small things like meeting the other children in her neighborhood were keys to success. Katie tells me "It's a 'no' unless you ask" and she learned that living life alone or with a support system is a choice.

After leaving her husband and finding a safe place to live, Katie applied for and was accepted into the Women's Bean project, a social enterprise that provides transitional employment for chronically unemployed and impoverished women. Less than two years later, Katie is now employed and attending college, has stable housing, and her child is attending preschool.

What makes Katie different from so many other people just like her? Katie shares that being open to changing her life from day one and her ability to self-reflect are what made her turn-around possible.

I first met Katie when she was sharing her story in front of a room of several hundred people—her strength in sharing her story brought tears to my eyes. The challenges I have faced pale in comparison, and yet the lessons have been the same. Take care of yourself first. Keep trying until you get what you are after. Let go of the familiar and embrace the opportunity to step into the unknown. There is darkness before the sunrise.

In-depth training from Kelly on Chapter 8 is available here: http://kellyrobbins.net/tynsadvancedmaterial/

The advanced material will give you access to a training video from Kelly, a recap of the chapter, a top tip from the chapter and a challenge for you!

Work along with the book in the *Trust Your Next Step Workbook* http://kellyrobbins.net/trust-next-step-workbook/

CHAPTER 9

DO YOU HAVE THE RIGHT GEAR FOR YOUR TRIP?

THE TRAVELER SEES WHAT HE SEES. THE TOURIST SEES WHAT HE
HAS COME TO SEE.

G.K. CHESTERTON

Just as you would not go skiing without the right gear (you can get frostbite if you're not careful), there are several things you can do to prepare for an easy journey cutting Fresh Tracks. Warm gloves, snow pants, a jacket, and a helmet are the basics when on the slopes. If you're not a cold weather fan you may want some heated boots, glove warmers and a neck warmer. If you are skiing in the back country you may add a GPS, avalanche gear and friends who are experienced skiers.

The same is true as you set out on your journey to cut Fresh Tracks. Begin your preparations for this adventure *knowing* you will accomplish this goal, waiting for the opportunity of your next step to present itself, and staying prepared to handle what you didn't see coming.

In order to pack, it's helpful to have some idea of the terrain you'll be covering, including where you are starting from.

You have your map from Chapter 2 and have some idea of where you are and where you want to go. My journey quitting my corporate job looked like this:

I am working at a corporate job and feel stressed and out of balance both professionally and personally. My goal is to work from home, have the flexibility to run my kids around when I want and make a similar income. I would like to use my gifts of writing, communicating and marketing to maintain a sense of "Kelly the professional."

Your tracks probably look very different. Your tracks may lead down a road to better health, a bigger or better house, more frequent travel, or finding a life partner. Since you don't know where your journey will lead, you can't be completely ready for every encounter you'll have, however, you can take some initial steps to prepare for your journey based on what you do know.

Let's use the analogy of taking a backpack on your ski trip. You have to carry it all day, so you don't want to pack too much. You also want to make sure you have everything you'll need based on what you can expect to encounter, such as an extra pair of gloves in case yours get wet (major crash) and an energy bar and some water. If you are backpacking in the mountains of Wyoming in the summer, you will require much different gear than for a snowshoeing trip in the winter.

There are ultimately three basic rules for packing: don't overpack, wear layers, and know your basic survival gear.

RULE #1 – DON'T OVERPACK

You don't know how long your journey will be so it may be a natural instinct to want to bring everything you own. The thing is, you have to carry this pack every step of the way and you don't want too much stuff slowing you down. The intention is to leave as much baggage behind as you can and to travel lightly. Also realize that as you travel you will get to know yourself better and your needs will change. You will learn new things about yourself and you may be able to set some things down that you needed when you started but don't need anymore. As you recognize these items, take them out of your pack, set them down, and continue on cutting your Fresh Tracks freer, lighter and wiser than before. For now let's take a look at some of the things you will want to leave behind right from the start.

COMPARING YOURSELF TO OTHERS.

When you are comparing yourself to someone else you are judging, and someone is ending up better than another. My experience is I give myself the short stick. The truth is, I don't really know what's going on in the other person's life, and outside appearances can be deceiving. So I am comparing things I don't know much about anyway.

How do you stop comparing yourself to others?

Be sure to take time each week to celebrate your own successes. This is important! If you are anything like me, I tend to notice all the bad things about myself and my mind will focus in on those negatives and get stuck there. It takes focus and discipline to switch that habit. I start of every coaching call with celebrations. It's interesting because in the beginning, many people struggle to have anything to celebrate; that's how hard they are on themselves. And often within a few months their celebrations are easy to rattle off and they have a long list! Even if it's a small step, recognize the tracks you are making.

Be genuinely happy for others when they have a success. Life is so different now than it was 20 years ago. Social media in particular has made comparing lives an easy and consistent event. When you find yourself slipping down the rabbit hole of comparison, remember everyone posts only their happy moments on social media. Not the struggle or pain that got them there. Not the hours of tears they shed the night before. Social media is not a complete picture of reality.

I saw a great saying on Facebook the other day that I strive to embrace "You can always tell who the strong women are. They are the ones building one another up instead of tearing each other down." Do this in action! Buy your friends products. Support their adventures. Love their babies. Forward their events. Don't be jealous—be the first in line to encourage them on. Support, don't compare.

When I was a fledgling copywriter starting out in my own business, I subscribed to every free newsletter I could find. Every copywriting guru had their spin on things and I was soaking it all in. After a few years in business I was feeling like a real failure—I was in no way even close to their successful multi-million dollar writing projects or million dollar information products they produced. Some of them seemed to write a book every six months too!

I started unsubscribing to their e-zines one-by-one. And sure enough I started recognizing my successes more often and feeling better about myself—because I stopped comparing myself to them.

The truth is, I learned a lot from each of those experts in the beginning of my career. A point came when rather than learning from them I started comparing myself to them—and I was not them. My definition of success was much different than theirs. This single mom of three had no desire to focus on building a million-dollar empire. I wanted to volunteer at Brownies, focus on what to make for dinner and how to get two kids to different places at the same time. I was successful at it and I was achieving my goals.

Fifteen years later my goals and my definition of success have changed significantly. I realize that setting measurable goals for myself and focusing on achieving those is much more conducive to my success than comparing myself to the thousands of other coaches out there. Not comparing yourself with others means recognizing the truth that there is enough for everyone, and life is not a rush. Enjoy YOUR journey and celebrate theirs.

COMPETING WITH OTHERS

Similar to comparing yourself to someone else, when competing with other people, one person comes out ahead and one comes out behind. This is not the point of cutting Fresh Tracks! Have you ever listened to an interview with a true athlete? They are always competing, but it's with one person—themselves.

We are talking about your life here; it's not a competition and it's not a race. Keep the focus inward, not outward. When you view success based on your own efforts, winning/losing, having more than your neighbor or out-earning your high school classmates become irrelevant.

In Colorado we have mountains that are higher than 14,000 feet; we call them fourteeners (there are 54 of them). One year I had set a goal for myself to hike up five of them. The first one I hiked was Mt. Bierstadt and I went with two friends early one morning. My friends hiked for about an hour and decided to stop. I continued on. I drank a lot of water to stay hydrated, as people had recommended at that high altitude, and felt fully prepared to conquer the first of my five mountains. The climb went on and on and was beautiful. At one point I thought I had reached the top because I couldn't see any higher and I was so excited! I got to "the top" and realized I was about one quarter of the way there! In front of me was a huge mountain that looked to be made of solid rock and people were walking in single file, slowly up to the top! I was already getting tired and having difficulty breathing in the higher altitude. I realized when I had passed tree line (trees don't grow above about 11,000-12,000 feet) that I was in fact making it. I also recognized I was beginning to have a hard time breathing.

I kept going for another hour and felt like I had barely made any progress. That big mountain of rock was still far ahead! And then I realized I had to go to the bathroom… and there were no trees from here to the top. I walked for as long as I could hold it and then sat down off to the side to evaluate my options. I could pee in front of everyone but I was way too self-conscious to do that (what was everyone else doing? And why did no one tell me about this issue?) I made the executive decision to go back down and figure out what I missed in this important matter of relieving myself.

I attempted my second fourteener two weeks later and this time I was much better prepared. I made sure to empty my bladder as frequently as possible before tree line and had friends with me who were more likely to reach the top. I had two of my daughters with me on this hike, and my hiking buddy was experienced and brought three of her daughters. I figured we could hold our coats up to hide each other while we peed, if necessary.

On this hike I was completely shocked that people in their 70's were actually running up the mountain and passing me. Others were riding their bikes up the mountain. In fact, almost everyone was passing me and I was embarrassed. Trying to breathe while hiking with my friend, I realized how slowly I hiked and felt bad because I was slowing everyone down. As I was whining in embarrassment on the way up, one older man who was passing me turned and said, "The goal is to make it, not race it." He turned around and just kept on going in front me.

I heard him, and between gasps of air nodded my head in thanks. I started paying attention to different things. Sure enough, there were tons of people turning around, not making it to the top. Some of them were amazingly only 300 feet, even 100 feet from the top! Yes, I could barely breathe at that elevation and it literally took 15 minutes to go 100 feet. But you know what, I did make it to the top that day (and found a place to sneak and go to the bathroom up there too) and yes, we were one of the last groups to get back to our car.

That man made a simple comment to me in passing, yet it is so incredibly profound for so many areas of my life. Creating your Fresh Tracks is not a race or a competition. In fact, all of life is not a competition. The goal is to make it, not race it. If you want to make it, you have to find your pace and stick with it, not someone else's.

WORRY

There's a saying "worry weighs a person down" and I take that literally. Worry is heavy and leads to anxiety and often health issues, including weight gain.

Are you aware how much of your time you spend worrying? Remember the Universal Law of Thinking? What we think about expands, so it makes sense to spend time paying attention to what we are thinking about.

Once I started paying attention, I found I was spending focused time each morning grounding in on my goals and I felt great that I completed my spiritual practice for the day. And then, the minute I stopped concentrating, worry popped into my head uninvited. Not only was I not conscious of the worrying I was doing most of the time, but I reversed all the good seed planting I did earlier.

From my knees that are making noises and hurt after I ski, to my teenage daughter's driving lessons, I was worrying more than I wanted to admit.

Two things I know for sure:

1. What I focus on expands (whether the focus is conscious or not doesn't matter).

2. The "seeds" or thoughts I plant today are what manifests for me tomorrow.

Once I became aware of some of the worrying I was doing, I stopped and looked at parts of my life that I didn't like. Was I worrying these areas into existence, and if so, what's the opposite that I do want?

In this Fresh Tracks with Kelly Robbins podcast, I teach in-depth on many facets of worrying, and I discuss worrying about debt, wealth, abundance, lack, need and specifically money. Listen here for the full training if any of that sounds intriguing! http://www.freshtrackswithkellyrobbins.com/being-in-business/worrying-manifesting-disaster/

DID YOU KNOW THAT THE HISTORY OF THE WORD WORRY MEANS TO CHOKE OR STRANGLE?

The truth is that when we worry, it's about things that either happened in the past and we can't do anything about, or we are worrying about the future, which hasn't happened yet, and in fact is planting the seeds of the future. We are creating what we don't want to happen rather than what we do!

Is there a secret key to help us stop worrying? I don't believe there is a one-size fits all answer. However, taking 100 percent responsibility for what we have manifested in our life, and taking control of our thoughts as frequently as possible (which is work) is imperative to success.

Choose to become aware. Make the statement "I choose to be aware" out loud and say it repeatedly. Be willing to change. Willing to see where you are out of alignment with truth. This is where the transformation begins.

You don't want to carry the heavy weight of worry when you cut Fresh Tracks.

Over-Controlling

The need to control can be a tough one to overcome, yet is a key factor to allowing life to flow through you rather than forcing it to be a certain way. There is an amazing book by David R. Hawkins called *Power vs. Force*, which does an excellent job explaining the difference between creating from a place of flow versus forcing a specific outcome.

There is a balance between taking action towards achieving your goals and holding on tightly, controlling every step, every breath and every outcome. You cannot control how everything unfolds, and you are not supposed to. Learn to surrender. Your future is unpredictable—it's supposed to be. You can handle it! Trust yourself. Trust your next step.

When you find yourself becoming over-controlling there is an underlying reason. It's often fear of something. If you find this is an issue for you, like it has been for me, take a breath and try to discover what it is you are afraid of. When you are controlling you may feel more secure, but in reality you are holding on tight and blocking the flow. The flow of creativity, the flow of life, the flow of energy.

The only way to change this behavior is to catch yourself in the act (or have a friend point it out for you) and then look at the underlying feelings behind it. Watch your behavior for a few days and see if you catch yourself micromanaging, obsessively worrying, being overly critical, overprotective, overplanning or doing anything you feel like you can't resist. Just stop and feel into why. What emotion are you struggling with? It may seem like you are engaging in these behaviors to reduce stress, but it's actually what's causing the stress.

Once you uncover the emotion, challenge your thinking. Is this logical reasoning or emotional reasoning? Then do the opposite of what you want to do.

The only thing you can actually control is yourself. Once you are in control of you, it's easy to trust yourself.

BAD HABITS

Bad habits can make or break your success as a Fresh Tracker. We all have habits, both good and bad, and some of them are easier to change than others.

Let's start by first looking at what a habit is, how it's different than the 35,000 decisions the average person makes in a day, and then examine which ones we want to keep or let go of.

A decision is the choice you make about something after thinking about it. Whereas a habit is a learned behavior that has become nearly or completely involuntary.

Is that glass of wine (or three) you have every night a decision or a habit? What about that five dollar Starbucks? The two hours on social media every night? The run you take each morning? The truth is 40 percent of "decisions" we make every day aren't decisions, they are habits.

HOW TO CHANGE HABITS

Something triggers every habit and every habit has a function. For example, mindless eating might help you comfort yourself emotionally. Watching TV for hours each night may allow you to hide from an unhealthy relationship. There are three stages to a habit; prompt, routine, reward.

If you want to change a habit, start by taking a personal look at what the reward is.

Is it feeling in control? Because of this need to be in control you have a habit of checking your email first thing in the morning and every fifteen minutes all day so all your clients' needs have been met before you do something for yourself. What's important to recognize is what craving your habit is really satisfying.

The routine is easy to discover and it's usually what we want to change. The cookie at break time. Checking your emails. Time spent on Facebook.

In order to successfully change a habit, the reward has to stay the same and you replace it with another routine.

The prompt or trigger is what starts the habit process. Being tired after a long day is a prompt (the reward you give yourself may be having a drink with friends after work). Feeling empty watching television alone at night is a prompt (reward is spending time on social media).

Countless studies have shown that a prompt and a reward, on their own, aren't enough for a new habit to last. Only when your brain starts expecting the reward—craving the good feeling or sense of accomplishment—will it become automatic to hop into your workout shoes and complete the five mile run. The prompt, in addition to triggering a routine, must also trigger a craving for the reward to come.

Want to change some bad habits? In addition to the prompt, routine, reward process, here are a few tips to help you set yourself up for success:

▶ Visualize yourself succeeding

▶ Surround yourself with people who live the way you want to live

▶ Cut out as many triggers as possible (if you smoke when you drink, don't drink for a while)

▶ Print out a calendar and put big X on each day you accomplish it

▶ Be disciplined

My intention for this teaching on habits is that you take an honest look at your life and how you are living. For more on habits, author Charles Duhigg has a book *The Power of Habit: Why We Do What We Do in Life and Business* that discusses this in depth. What can, should, or needs to change for you to create your Fresh Tracks? Here are a just a few samplings of habits many successful people have in common. Perhaps some of these will help inspire you.

Habits of successful people

▶ Plan out their day the night before

▶ Read inspirational books

▶ Make their health a priority

▶ Don't get distracted by what other people are doing

▶ Disciplined to work even when don't want to

▶ Learn to quiet their minds—even for 15 minutes

▶ Batch check emails twice a day

The place to look right now: are any of your habits detrimental to you achieving your goal? How can you tell if it's a bad habit you need to change? Part of you will just know. If you're not sure, ask if it's impairing the ability of your new habit to take root. This means taking an honest look at yourself and implementing the power of your word. Start with small changes and more forward from there.

Lack of integrity

Integrity means doing the right thing, even if no one is watching. It means being true to yourself and doing nothing that demeans or dishonors you.

When you lack integrity you will struggle to maintain strong relationships, you'll waiver when other people's opinions differ from yours, and when crisis hits you'll find you won't weather the storm and you turn to others for help. You don't trust yourself because you don't have all the tools you need. You are not in control and disciplined in the living of *you*.

Because you change your word frequently, you don't trust yourself and others don't trust you. Your self-esteem and your personal strength is weak and you bend and sway with the opinion of others rather than listening to yourself.

How do you become a person of integrity?

1. Make few promises and keep the ones you do make.

2. Be direct and appreciate truth. Surrounding yourself with "yes" people does not serve you—only your ego. Be open to hearing the truth and be one who says it.

3. Don't cheat. Cheaters never win and if you do win it is in the short-term and never for the ultimate good.

4. Be impeccable with your word. It is the first of *The Four Agreements*, a must read classic by Don Miguel Ruiz for everyone on the journey of self-discovery. Impeccable is a strong word if you think about it! Start paying attention to your word and how often you, as Dr. Seuss said, "say what you mean and mean what you say", both to others and yourself.

5. Live your values.

RULE #2 – WEAR LAYERS

Ask any Coloradoan and they will tell you to dress in layers. The weather can change in an instant, along with the elevation and surroundings. If you want to enjoy yourself and make it through the day in comfort, it's important you are comfortable in your ever changing surroundings. You must be able to adapt.

This may mean starting the day out with two layers of shirts, a hoodie and a hat. And then taking off two of the layers by lunchtime. And then putting one of the layers back on in the early afternoon when the sun goes behind the clouds for a few hours. And then adjusting again when the sun is beating on your back an hour later. Because you are equipped properly, you can easily adjust to the changing conditions and focus on enjoying your day—not the constantly changing weather.

When I left corporate America my goal was to work from home, be with my kids, and use my communication and writing skills. Freelance copywriting fit that description. So did creating The Copywriting Institute a few years later. And so does the coaching, speaking and teaching I do now. If I had focused on writing websites exclusively and not been open to the changing opportunities that presented themselves to me along the way, I would still be writing copy. Instead I've grown and expanded and helped the world in a bigger and better way over the years. I didn't hold on tightly to the "how;" I made my living as long as my ultimate goals were being met.

The key to successfully creating Fresh Tracks is staying in a constant state of adaptability. Adaptability starts with maintaining an open mind and recognizing opportunity as it presents itself. Taking on new challenges rather than avoiding them and being willing to enter new domains as they appear are the only ways to grow, and they require you to adapt. By learning to adapt you will find you ultimately react to change better and are less likely to worry and start a downward spiral of despair.

How do you learn to adapt? By being attentive to what's going on, having a vision for what you intend to create, and cultivating flexibility. These are all important traits for the adaptable Fresh Tracker.

One of the fastest ways we prevent adaptability is by being rigid and controlling. We make a plan and lay out how we are going to accomplish that plan and don't waiver in how we accomplish it. We rationalize that we planned it this way for a reason and are determined to follow through with it, thinking we are being resilient. In fact, we are forcing how we accomplish our goals rather than adapting to perhaps better ways of accomplishing them.

You can't force the "how" and it's not your job to. It's your job to be open and see the opportunity as it presents itself to you. We are not taught to do this with our lives and often don't see the opportunity that is right before our eyes because it doesn't look the way we think it should.

When we focus on our goals and aren't attached to HOW they unfold, we open ourselves to even greater opportunities than we could have imagined. You can be prepared by being flexible—wearing layers. If you get hot you take off a layer or two. Cool down put a layer back on. Layers allow you to remain comfortable, flexible, and adaptable so you can continue on your journey.

Rule #3 – Pack Basic Survival Gear

A strong foundation is critical when you build anything. Packing the basics like water, food and sunscreen is mandatory in order to safely stay outside for more than a few hours. Your basic survival gear for cutting Fresh Tracks is one area where there is most often room for improvement, it involves layers of consciousness and change, and requires constant upkeep.

MENTAL AND EMOTIONAL WELLNESS

Your mental health is the number one thing that will make or break your success on your journey. Being a mentally and emotionally healthy person is more than not being depressed or anxious. It's the way you feel about yourself, the quality of the friendships you have, how well you handle stress and bounce back from setbacks. The meaning and joy you bring to life as well as your contribution and connection to community are part of your mental and emotional set point.

In order to trust yourself and your next step, you need to know yourself. It's surprising how many people really don't know themselves—even though most would say they do. People avoid getting to know who they really are because looking inside can be scary.

I encourage you to be open and honest with yourself and step into consciously learning who you are, what you believe and why. Don't continue to go through life simply because it's the way you always have. Because that is the way everyone else is doing it. Most of society goes through their lives reacting rather than responding—this is not how you are going to create anything!

When we react we are letting emotions without reason move us forward. Reacting is usually sporadic and based in emotion, not logic. Responding is a completely different scenario. Responses contain reasoning and are more thoughtful. Moving from the default state of reacting to situations rather than responding to them can be a process. It may be easier to transition to this default state when you have a team in your corner guiding you.

Be open to getting help and don't worry about what anyone else thinks about it. Investigate twelve step programs, delve into forgiveness work, discover how to release pent-up anger, even go to therapy if that's what it takes to get a good look inside yourself. Be conscious about what you put in your mind. Read thought-provoking books rather than trashy novels, attend interesting workshops, overall make an effort to be around people who are different than you.

You may know some people who have hit rock bottom and then turned their life around. The truth about that is their life had to be so completely miserable that they were willing to do whatever it took to make changes. Life had to get completely miserable and intolerable for them to make the tough changes they needed to make. It does not have to be that way.

Being mentally and emotionally healthy is a choice and it is hard work. It can take discipline, courage and determination. You want to get to the place where you don't care what anyone else thinks about you or what you do, and you know that you will take the action steps necessary to change your life. For you to create your own emotional wellness without hitting rock-bottom will require you to cultivate within yourself a sense of urgency. A sense of determination. A sense of "bring it on, I'm ready for it now!!"

POSITIVE MINDSET

Is positive mindset an overused buzz word you've heard 50 million times? Don't skip over this section quite yet! This popular term keeps popping up for a reason—and the truth is that maintaining a positive mindset, particularly when cutting Fresh Tracks, is not a natural state for most of us and we have to focus on it.

If you've struggled with saying your positive affirmations three times a day, if you know from personal experience that meditating is truthfully a great time to think through your shopping list, and you've done the positive-statements-on-a-sticky-note-on-the-bathroom-mirror thing and find it silly, I'm with you. I've been there. It feels like a waste of time, sounds better than it really is and doesn't work. Deep down you know that affirmations are a bunch of happy crap and you don't need to focus on these things because you are serious and mean business! There's action to be taken and tasks to be accomplished!

Hold on… I caution you not to write it all off just yet. While the methods may seem fluffy and ineffective, the truth is that expecting positive outcomes versus negative outcomes does make a difference in both how we feel and what we can expect to receive.

You are in charge of your life. You are the energy that runs your machine, both physically and mentally, and no one else can feed that machine but you. YOU have choice. Always. Be aware of what you put in your machine and every day take specific action to be positive in your thoughts, your awareness, and your expectations. In time you'll find what comes out is more positive than what was coming out in the past. You'll find your relationships with your partner, your children, and your professional contacts are more positive. You'll even find more positive people wanting to be around you because like attracts like. Have you heard the saying "garbage in garbage out?" That concept applies to your mind and your thoughts just as much as a computer science problem.

HOW DO I BECOME A MORE POSITIVE PERSON?

Simply asking yourself that question is a great place to start. Then begins a process of self-discovery and finding what motivates you. Here are a few ideas. Try listening to different speakers on YouTube or Ted talks. Are you a reader? There are hundreds of thousands of authors with both audio and written books that are motivational. Podcasts are another alternative. They're free and provide a consistent variety of both content and speakers.

The information and opportunity is available to expose yourself to different ideas, different ways of viewing life, and much of it is free or low-cost. It's your job to continuously feed this information to yourself and monitor your information intake.

One of the first things I have my private clients do is stop reading novels. Many of them are readers, like me, and because they are embarking on such a big leap, I have them intentionally go inward and focus on what they are putting in their minds.

I am an avid reader and love my novels and I literally have hundreds on my bookshelf. I now save them for vacations and when I am in desperate need of a break. Which is a few times a year. I still read every day, but I'm conscious to not put "garbage in" except as a treat. There is a difference in value between a trashy novel and a book that helps you grow.

The same is true for television and movies. Again, be cautious what you are putting in, particularly right before bed. When I was going through my first major life breakthrough I completely quit watching television. I loved Law and Order SVU and would often watch it right before I went to sleep. I was reading and studying a book about Faith and what that meant to me and I realized I'm regularly watching a show about children getting hurt. This was not in alignment with how I was working to feel positive and empowered each day! I quit TV for a while. I now watch it but make conscious choices in which shows I'm watching and how I'm feeling after watching them. A friend of mine has taken to watching Ted talks on his iPad before bed instead of the news.

Finally, the people you surround yourself with play an important role in how you feed yourself. We went in-depth on relationships in Chapter 6. Take a look at who you spend your time with, how you feel after you are with them, and the energy they "put out" into the world.

MENTOR OR COACH

You have to do it yourself, but you don't have to do it alone.

So far we've talked about creating a lot of change in your life, from making choices about your friends and who you surround yourself with to pulling up and examining long-held, hidden beliefs and attitudes. Creating Fresh Tracks is about to stir things up in your world.

While no one can take these steps for you, it can be helpful to have someone more experienced than you available to guide you, answer questions honestly, and help you see what's going on clearly rather than through whatever lens you see through. Corporations often have formal mentorship programs for employees. Replicating that situation in others areas of your life is done by hiring a coach. Coaches specialize in all sorts of areas such as health, spirituality, career, business, wealth coaching, etc.

How do you know if you should hire a coach?

▶ You lack confidence

▶ Feel unclear on your vision or where you want to go on your map

▶ Your habits don't support your goals

▶ You feel overwhelmed

▶ Your vision feels too big

▶ You are in a transition and your friends and family aren't the support you need

▶ You have been working hard to accomplish a goal and you feel like nothing is happening

▶ You want to speed up your results and reduce mistakes

A favorite quote of mine by Albert Einstein says "Problems cannot be solved by the same level of thinking that created them." Your job is to do what you need to do to change the level of thinking that has you where you are today, particularly if you are feeling stuck. Getting guidance from someone outside your day-to-day world can be enlightening, freeing and help you reduce time spent feeling your way down the wrong path.

Another way to look at coaching is to consider the quality of questions you ask yourself. Having a trusted person ask questions—particularly ones you and the people in your sphere of influence don't know to ask—can be a complete game changer. You don't know what you don't know. Question asking is a great way to get there.

OPENNESS

What does it mean to be open? It's more than being open-minded, it's a state of being.

Let's start with what "being" means. The study of the nature of being is an actual thing. It's called ontology. How you are being is different than what you are feeling and the emotions you experience. It is how you present in situations.

One example is whether you are being open or being closed. To be open is being available to receive (this could be receiving information, tangible things such as gifts and money, or the truth). Being open is imperative to creating Fresh Tracks because if you want to create something different, you need to be able to see your world in a different light. We spoke earlier about the lens we view the world through. Being open to even acknowledge there may be a different way to view the situation is an important start. Being open that you always have a choice, even if you don't like the choice, is being open.

I also believe being open is an energetic way of being. It's more than being open-minded. You choose to be open to seeing your true self. Be open to be authentic and, warts and all, love yourself.

It's a choice to be open to see, recognize and trust your next step. You are more likely to look for and see different ways to approach a problem when you are open as opposed to being closed. Allowing ourselves more options allows more solutions to be available to us. Limiting ourselves to what we have known to be true in the past has kept us comfortable and getting uncomfortable is an important aspect in creating Fresh Tracks.

I have found one of the most important places to remain open (and that I have had to work the hardest at) is being open about learning the true nature of myself. Receiving feedback can be tough! When we are digging into such personal aspects of ourselves as our beliefs, how we are showing up in the world, how others see us, being open to receive the truth is imperative for us to grow into the person we need to be to get to our next place in life. That's why hiring a coach or mentor can be so valuable. A coach is not family or friends with an agenda and personal history with you. They are here to reflect the truth back to you. Being open to discovering the real you, the authentic you, and not taking the negatives personally but using the information as tools to guide your adjustments in working with Universal Law can help speed up change and reduce the uncertainty in your journey.

CUSTOMIZED GEAR FOR YOUR TRIP

Each journey to creating Fresh Tracks is unique. As individuals we have to take an objective look at what is truly necessary to pack and what we would simply like to have because it reduces stress. When skiing, sometimes in order to be comfortable we'll opt to upgrade to heated ski boots or have the boots custom fitted. You will need to make decisions like this for your life as you step forward. My friend George loves skiing and is from the hot, southern part of the United States. He loves snow skiing but does not tolerate the cold well, so he had custom heaters installed in his ski boots. He knows himself enough that in order to enjoy a sport he truly loves, he needed to make himself comfortable and be warm.

How does this apply to you and your journey? Each journey creating Fresh Tracks is different. You'll have to take an honest look at what is important enough for you to do that you need to customize your ride.

It's easy to fall prey to low self-esteem, which rears its ugly head often, and many feel the need to build their confidence by becoming over-qualified. Watch out for this sneaky, low-confidence trick we do to ourselves by overeducating and underdoing!

SPECIFIC TRAINING AND ADVANCED DEGREES

Getting yet another degree pops up often and is often not necessary. If you are a clerk in a grocery store and your map takes you down the astrophysics path, yes, you will probably need to get that degree under your belt. If your path is taking you down a corporate path then yes, a degree or an advanced degree will probably help you.

However, most of us do not need to go back to college to create our Fresh Tracks. Take a hard look before you do this. I have spoken with so many adults with PhDs and multiple degrees who are still searching for their purpose and taking that next step in their life. They are over-educated and under-contributing to life. I am going to ask you to take an honest look at whether you truly need to invest in more certifications, degrees, or training.

Here is an exercise to help you make the decision to move forward with training or advanced schooling:

1. Make a list of all your skills, especially those that may apply to where you want to go. If you have a friend or mentor you respect, ask that person for feedback on this list too. We tend to underestimate our accomplishments or not see the big-picture. Make a comprehensive list of your true skills.

2. Make a separate list of what you imagine you need to get you where you want to be. You may need to do some research here. Find someone who is already there and ask, or look up biographies of people who have accomplished something similar and see what their path looked like. Remember, life is NOT a cookie-cutter formula.

3. What do you need to take your next step only? Do not make big picture decisions here. If your goal is to become a personal chef and teach busy, health-minded people how to cook their own healthy meals, your first step may be to start cooking healthy foods for yourself. Or to price five meals— what do the ingredients cost? How long does it take to purchase the food and prepare it? Would you teach them how to shop for their own food and if so how much more would that cost? Are there any other people in your area who do this? Ask how much training is really needed.

One of the things I did when I quit my corporate job and started my freelance copywriting business was go to graduate school. In corporate America I was behind some of my peers and made less because I did not have a master's degree. Those feelings of insecurity and of being "less than" followed me when I started my own business. My thoughts were, "Who will hire me as a business owner if I am not even on-par with the average Joe in corporate?" I'm glad I did it, however, it was without question not necessary. No one, not even once, has asked me about my education since I started my business. Not once. It was money I didn't have that was unnecessarily spent because of my low self-esteem.

I share this advice because I believe it to be true and an important step many take that is not necessary. I also want to say I am firm believer in always learning and continuing to grow and that can be through both formal and informal education. In fact, I am right now taking classes once a week and am always reading books and attending workshops—growth is good.

The point here is to evaluate if you NEED more training, another certificate, a college degree, etc. to achieve your Fresh Tracks. Don't let your insecurities send you down a side road. Make your journey to creating Fresh Tracks as clean and simple as possible.

As you can see, having the right gear for your trip is essential to enjoying the ride creating Fresh Tracks. Remember the three basic rules for packing: don't overpack, wear layers, and know your basic survival gear.

In-depth training from Kelly on Chapter 9 is available here: http://kellyrobbins.net/tynsadvancedmaterial/

The advanced material will give you access to a training video from Kelly, a recap of the chapter, a top tip from the chapter and a challenge for you!

Work along with the book in the *Trust Your Next Step Workbook* http://kellyrobbins.net/trust-next-step-workbook/

A LAST WORD

You've made the decision to start living a full life. You've created your personal trail map and examined where your life is currently. Additionally, you've done some planning and dreaming about where you want to take it next. You know what tools you have to work with and have been exposed to what types of gear to pack and what to leave behind on your journey to make it as light and smooth as possible.

You are now ready to create Fresh Tracks. You are ready to find The Edge and grow beyond what you've done before.

Now is absolutely the time to move forward. The world desperately needs Fresh Trackers such as yourself to change the way we live our lives. To break the mold of mediocrity and boredom so many of us have accepted as normal. To show both ourselves and others how to live our lives as fully, expressively, and abundantly as possible. To break through the bondage of numbness that has taken over so much of our society today.

On an intimate level I want you to understand that the change you seek in this world starts with you. If you yearn for a more peaceful existence, for more abundance, for more love, less drama, more honesty and openness in relationships, more integrity in business interactions, more laughter, health and the enjoyment that comes from living on purpose and feeling connected with others... the change starts with you. Only you have control of yourself, no one else.

I implore you to not wait for the stars to align perfectly before you get started—they won't. You can't wait for your partner or you parents or your kids to go first. The President, your boss, and other leaders in the community—they won't go first. They will not hold your hand or beg and plead for you to live the full and wonderful life you are entitled to live.

The change starts with you and only you.

Your job, and it's easy to say your most important job, is to dream, create and step into cutting your Fresh Tracks. Now. Today. Right this moment. No one can live your life for you. No one else can or will stir up that internal longing, the urgency and energy needed to live the life you are designed to live. No one else can hear or feel the internal messages and nudges you feel. They are meant for you and you alone.

Listen to them. Act on them. Trust yourself.

Taking 100 percent responsibility for everything in your life allows you to begin to look introspectively and to not only take ownership but responsibility for how you choose to experience this life.

We talked quite a bit about The Edge. Know that The Edge keeps coming—it is not a one-time thing. My experience is that the first time crossing The Edge is the hardest because you don't know how or where or when the scariness of the unknown will stop. The uncomfortableness of pushing yourself beyond what you've ever done before seems never ending. You don't know when or if the discomfort will end.

Know that once you have survived crossing The Edge the first time, the second time becomes easier. Not because it is any less scary or painful than the first time, but because you've experienced it once before and you know what it is and that it will end. You may recognize what is happening as you are in the throes of it and that may bring some peace. Some confidence.

I encourage you to dream and dream big. Learn to listen to yourself and honor your thoughts and experiences. Be brave. Reach out for help. Find others who are on a similar journey—you don't have to go it alone. Let go of beliefs, friends and anything else that no longer serves you. Prepare yourself to be the best you you are capable of being. And do it today.

Let's go cut some Fresh Tracks!

ACKNOWLEDGMENTS

I would first like to thank my family. For their unwavering encouragement, their understanding of the time I spent away from them with my nose in the computer and for ignoring my mumbling and grumbling as I played with a thought that wasn't coming through quite clearly for a few days on end. I love each of you more than you can imagine.

I am also incredibly grateful for my many editors and their unbridled feedback; Shelby Robbins, Brooke Harris Martellaro, Dr. Ras Smith, Shirley Woodrum, and the Motivational Press team. This book would not be what it is without each of you and your unique insights. Questioning me and challenging me to push for more was exactly what I needed.

I am also grateful for my larger community of friends whose love, support and judgment-free reassurance that this book would get done kept me going. I felt your love! This book took twice as long to write as I had planned and more time than I ever imagined to edit.

Thank you to my friends and community at Mile High Church who supported me through tears and frustration, laughter and silliness and love. And my social media friends who cheered me on as I procrastinated and posted updates on my progress. Who kept me upbeat and smiling when I needed it. And finally, my besties at e-women, who helped lift me to be the woman I am today.

And finally to my man, George, for sticking by me and encouraging me when I was stressing out and doubting my next step. Thank you for trusting me. And for the wine, the getaways and the howling laughter when I need it.

BOOK CLUB QUESTIONS

1. What was the purpose of this book?

2. What was your biggest takeaway from this book?

3. Was there a specific passage that left an impression? What was the passage and the effect on you?

4. What Fresh Tracks have you cut in your past? Any that you are most proud of? Any that you regret?

5. Is there something you have always wanted to do but haven't? Have you avoided cutting Fresh Tracks in a specific area?

6. Did certain parts of the book make you uncomfortable? Why?

7. How does the issue of Trusting Your Next Step affect your life on a daily basis or in a more general sense?

8. Did you learn something new? Did it broaden your perspective on an issue?

9. What are your thoughts/experiences regarding the "living a numb life" discussion?

10. What are your thoughts about the teachings on Universal Law? Are any of them easier for you than others? Are any harder for you than others?

11. What changes, if any, are you ready to make in your life after reading this book?

12. How has reading this book changed your opinion of a certain person or topic?

13. What did you find surprising about the facts in this book?

ADDITIONAL FRESH TRACKS RESOURCES

- ▶ Podcast: www.FreshTrackswithKellyRobbins.com available on iTunes, iHeartRadio (free apps on Google play and Amazon)
- ▶ Dig deep into the exercises with the Trust Your Next Step Workbook http://kellyrobbins.net/trust-next-step-workbook/
- ▶ Advanced Material http://kellyrobbins.net/tynsadvancedmaterial/
- ▶ The Edge Newsletter www.KellyRobbins.net
- ▶ Living Numb Manifesto and self-assessment http://kellyrobbins.net/numblife/

ABOUT THE AUTHOR

 Former corporate employee turned entrepreneur, Kelly Robbins shares her inspirational message of self-leadership, personal power, and responsibility with Fresh Trackers around the world. Her work teaching Universal Law, coaching and writing supports her mission of supporting and inspiring others to freely express their talents and gifts in a fun and loving way.

Kelly lives outside of Boulder, Colorado with her man, George, her youngest daughter, Madilynn, her stepson Jack, and their golden retriever, Chewbacca. Kelly enjoys ditching everything to hit slopes on a snowy day, hiking in the nearby Rocky Mountains every chance she gets, and writing whenever possible. Kelly believes there is nothing like reading a good book snuggled by the fire on a cold day.

You can learn more about Kelly and the programs she offers at www.KellyRobbins.net.

CPSIA information can be obtained
at www.ICGtesting.com
Printed in the USA
FSHW012026170619
59163FS